THE LITTLE GUIDES
CATS

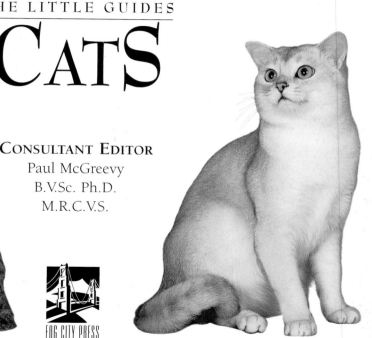

THE LITTLE GUIDES
CATS

CONSULTANT EDITOR
Paul McGreevy
B.V.Sc. Ph.D.
M.R.C.V.S.

FOG CITY PRESS

Published by Fog City Press
814 Montgomery Street
San Francisco, CA 94133 USA
Reprinted in 2000 (three times), 2001 (twice), 2002 (twice),
2003 (three times)

Chief Executive Officer: John Owen
President: Terry Newell
Publisher: Lynn Humphries
Managing Editor: Janine Flew
Design Manager: Helen Perks
Editorial Coordinator: Jennifer Losco
Production Manager: Caroline Webber
Production Coordinator: James Blackman
Sales Manager: Emily Jahn
Vice President International Sales: Stuart Laurence

Project Editor: Lynn Cole
Designers: Arne Falkenmire, Katie Ravich
Consultant Editor: Dr. Paul McGreevy

A catalog record for this book is available from
the Library of Congress, Washington, DC.

ISBN 1 875137 65 3

Color reproduction by Colourscan Co Pte Ltd
Printed by LeeFung-Asco Printers
Printed in China

A Weldon Owen Production

CONTENTS

PART THREE
CAT BREEDS

PART ONE

ALL ABOUT CATS

THE CAT

During the 35 million years the cat family has been on Earth, many new species have emerged, all with certain "catlike" traits. Today, there are 36 species of these amazing predators, including the domestic cat, and humans find them fascinating. All modern species of cats share a great many physical and genetic similarities because they are all descended from a single remote ancestral species. Cat species occur throughout the world but the greatest diversity of species is found in the tropics. Where several species are in competition for food in an area, they seem to work things out instinctively by hunting at different times of day or going after different types of prey.

THE HISTORY OF CATS

The cat family can trace its history back 35 million years. In comparatively recent times, the ancient Egyptians are known to have adopted cats for domestic use. Taken on long sea voyages because of their ability to control rodents aboard ships, cats gradually spread throughout the world.

If you traveled back in time, to a forest of 35 million years ago, you would instantly recognize a *Proailurus* stalking along a branch as a cat. An unusual breed, perhaps, but clearly a cat. This is the cat from which all extinct and living cats of the family Felidae are believed to have arisen, and even that long ago, the traits that make all cats superb predators were in place—stabbing teeth, powerful jaws, flesh-ripping claws, agile bodies with flexible limbs and excellent binocular vision.

Proailurus appeared at a time of great evolutionary activity, in which today's carnivore families evolved from a group of creatures called miacids. Miacids probably most resembled today's cat-like civets and genets. They diversified into two carnivorous subgroups—the New World branch (bears, dogs, seals, raccoons, weasels and sea lions), and the Old World branch (cats, hyenas, civets and mongooses).

The 36 living cat species, from 600-pound (270 kg) tigers to 2.5-pound (1 kg) black-footed cats, share an ancestor that is similar to an ocelot, called *Pseudailurus*, a descendant of *Proailurus*. This creature lived in Eurasia between 10 and 15 million years ago. From this ancestor, cats diversified and spread, leaving only Australia and Antarctica without native cats.

Spreading out Cats were among the most successful of all mammals in colonizing the Earth. Lions once occupied a larger area than any other mammal, from parts of South America, through North America, Asia, Europe and Africa. Wild cats, the ancestors of domestic cats, found homes from the southern tip of Africa to the farthest reaches of Europe and Asia. In the past 10,000 years, these magnificent predators have steadily lost ground to their only serious competitors, people.

Domestication How and at what period various species of wild cat became domesticated is hard to

TRACING THE FAMILY TREE

Recent molecular analyses reveal that modern cats evolved in three distinct lines. The largest, the pantherine line, led with 24 of the 36 species of living cats, including golden cats, servals, pumas, lynxes, cheetahs and all big cats. Another line led to the seven species of small South American cats; and the third line to the other species, including the domestic cat and its close relatives.

establish. While it is possible that cats dwelt in farming villages in the Middle East as long as 10,000 years ago, the only conclusive evidence, from ancient Egypt, is dated only to about 2000 BC.

As the way of life changed from nomadic to agrarian, people had to ensure that they had sufficient food supplies to last from one harvest to the next. Although the grain was kept in storehouses, it could never be fully protected against mice and rats that were able to sneak through cracks.

In their search for food, wild cats wandered into settlements, hunting and feeding on the increasingly abundant mice and rats. The farmers quickly realized how useful the cats were in killing the vermin and protecting their grain supplies and, unlike dogs, which had long been domesticated, cats were especially useful because they were predatory at night when the mice and rats were feeding. Rather than chasing the cats away, the farmers set about encouraging them to stay, first by feeding them and eventually by petting them. Not surprisingly, with an endless supply of food at hand and protection from their enemies, the cats became disinclined to wander back to the wild.

The cat family Until recently, the cat family, Felidae, was classified into three groups based on their similarities and differences: Big cats (*Panthera*) were grouped together because they are big and kill large prey. Small cats (*Felis*) were grouped together because they are relatively small and usually take small prey, although pumas, long included in this group, are quite big and take large prey. Cheetahs (*Acinonyx*), with their lanky bodies, unsheathed retractile claws, and adaptations for high speed, formed their own group. However, species can look very much alike not because they are closely related but because they are adapted to similar lifestyles. So by studying the genetic make-up of the cat family, scientists have reclassified them into eight groups, called lineages. The cats within each lineage are more closely related to

SKULL STRUCTURE
Stabbing teeth set in powerful jaws are a significant feature in the skulls of both the tiger and the domestic cat.

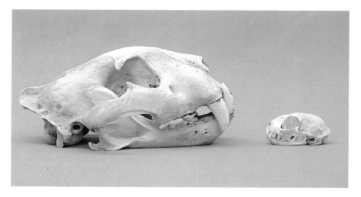

each other than to the cats in other lineages. The Panthera lineage consists of the six species of big cats—lions, tigers, jaguars, leopards, snow leopards and clouded leopards. The Ocelot lineage is made up of seven small South American cats—ocelots, margays, oncillas, pampas cats, Andean mountain cats, kodkod and Geoffrey's cats.

Then there is the Lynx lineage of lynxes, bobcats and, more surprisingly, the marbled cats of Asia, which, based on distribution, habits and physical appearance, were long thought to be a type of miniature clouded leopard.

The African caracal, with beautiful tufted ears, and the African golden cat form the Caracal lineage, while the latter's look-alike, the Asian golden cat, is grouped with the little-known Bornean bay cat in the Bay Cat lineage. Asia's fishing cats and flat-headed cats, both unusual in their ability to catch fish, the common leopard cat, and the rare

EAR MARKED
The African serval has an elongated profile because of its large, erect ears.

Iriomote cat, found only on the Pacific island of the same name, make up the Asian Leopard Cat lineage. Most surprising is the Puma lineage, which consists of that big "small cat" as well as the slinky jaguarundi and the cheetah.

Two species remain unclassified, the lanky, big-eared African serval, which specializes in pouncing on rodents as they emerge from underground burrows, and the rusty-spotted cat, a native of India and Sri Lanka that at less than three pounds rivals the black-footed cat for the title of world's smallest cat.

Finally, there is the Domestic Cat lineage, which groups your favorite pet and its wild ancestors with the

THE SACRED CAT
By 1500 BC, the cat was considered a sacred animal in Egypt and was represented in countless works of art.

tiny black-footed cat, the desert-dwelling sand cat, the long-furred, flat-faced Pallas cat of Asia, the plain-coated jungle cat and the rare Chinese mountain cat.

Demigod status It is thought that in about 1500 BC, the Pharaoh

of Egypt had a supply of grain of such magnitude that he needed more cats to protect it. Because the people were unwilling to part with their cats, it is believed that the Pharaoh proclaimed all cats demigods. This meant that a normal mortal had no rights to owning a

cat, while the Pharaoh, who was of divine status, did. The cats were still permitted to live in the homes of the people by day, but had to be brought to the storehouses at night to catch vermin.

Their new status ensured that cats were worshipped and pampered. Severe punishments were inflicted if a cat was harmed, and if one was killed, the punishment was death.

When a cat died, there was a period of mourning, after which the cat would be mummified. In an elaborate ceremony, it was buried in a wooden or bronze casket in a cat cemetery. Archeologists have found more than 300,000 cat mummies at one cemetery in Beni-Hassan, Egypt.

Sea voyages Sailors also needed to protect their grain and food supplies from mice and rats and so began to take cats with them on sea voyages. It is thought that Greek and Phoenician traders first took the domestic cat to the Middle East and present-day Italy in about 1000 BC.

Domestic cats were gradually introduced into Asia and Europe, eventually reaching England. They continued to be taken on ships and, as exploration and trade grew in importance in the 1600s, the cat spread throughout the New World.

Europe After being revered by the Romans as a symbol of liberty, the cat fell from grace in Europe for more than 200 years. In England, by the fourteenth century, the cat had come to symbolize evil and was closely associated with witchcraft and the Devil. Hundreds of thousands of cats were burned to death, with the Church not only condoning the slaughter but actually championing and encouraging it.

As cat populations dwindled, the rat population grew, culminating in the Black Death (bubonic plague) in 1334. This fatal disease, transmitted to people by rat fleas, quickly spread throughout Europe.

The cat's value in the control of rodents was rediscovered, and its popularity rapidly returned. By the late 1600s cat flaps were being installed in many households in France, so the family pet could come and go as it pleased.

Asia Cats are highly respected throughout Asia. In some regions, they were used in temples to protect manuscripts from rats and mice. They also helped guard the silkworm cocoons, the silk trade being of vital economic importance to China and Japan. (The silk trade was, in fact, so important to China that the talents of the silkworm were a well-kept secret for 3,000 years and anyone who let a careless word slip out faced a penalty of death.)

In Siam (present-day Thailand), cats could be owned only by royalty—the Siamese cat was once known as the royal cat of Siam.

CAT BIOLOGY AND ANATOMY

Felids are specialized in the sense that they are rather uniform in their hunting mode: solitary predators that stalk their prey, then attack in a brief rush. Most of their major anatomical features can be related to this typical predatory behavior.

The body of the cat The vertebral column must support the cat's body while still allowing great flexibility in movement. In the trunk region, it is like a taut bow, with the back muscles and belly muscles providing the tension that allows the cat's body to stretch and contract like a spring, for power and speed.

The teeth Dentition in cats is truly distinctive. The teeth are reduced in number, compared to other carnivores, and specialized in operation. Typically, there are 15 teeth on each side of the midline of the adult skull. These include, on each side, three upper and three lower incisors, one upper and one lower canine, three upper and two lower premolars, and one upper and one lower molar. The upper molar is comparatively small, and sometimes the most anterior premolar is very reduced or does not appear at all. Cat incisors are not unusual, but their canine teeth are large. In making a kill, the long, rounded canine teeth are inserted between the neck vertebrae of the victim.

In most terrestrial carnivores, the rearmost upper premolars and the most anterior lower molars are called carnassials. Carnassials have laterally flattened blades that shear past one another as the jaw is closed. The comparative extent of the carnassial blades depends on the preferred diet. Bear carnassials, for example, have low crowns, like ours, which make them better for crushing than for slicing. In cats, the carnassials are especially elongated,

SPECIALIZED HUNTERS

The skeletons of cats show variations on a common theme. In general, only the relative proportions of the various parts vary from species to species. Characteristics of the skull, such as length and breadth of canine teeth, are influenced by the diet of the particular species, while post-cranial traits, such as limb length, vary with the habitat-utilization patterns of the species.

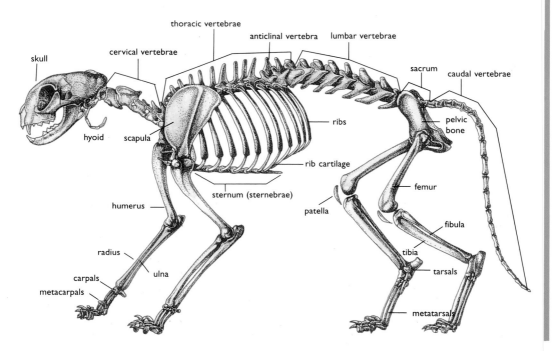

skull

cervical vertebrae

thoracic vertebrae

anticlinal vertebra

lumbar vertebrae

sacrum

caudal vertebrae

hyoid

scapula

ribs

pelvic bone

rib cartilage

sternum (sternebrae)

femur

humerus

patella

fibula

tibia

radius

ulna

tarsals

carpals

metacarpals

metatarsals

the crushing portions of the teeth are eliminated, and the other cheek teeth are either very small or are also modified blades.

The teeth each have a specialized task: the long canines grab and kill prey; the scissor-like molars, or carnassials, are used to tear chunks of meat from the carcass; and the small incisors remove every last morsel of meat from the bones.

The olfactory senses We don't know what information is conveyed by the cat's olfactory senses, and they have long been considered less acute than those of dogs. In addition to the usual nasal olfactory sensors, cats (and other carnivorans) have a vomeronasal organ, which is an auxiliary olfactory membrane located in paired canals leading from the roof of the mouth on each side, just behind the incisors. The sensory

functions of the organ are not thoroughly understood. It seems to be used by males when checking a female's breeding readiness.

Temperature control As in other carnivores, sweat glands are not abundant in cat skin. They are most concentrated in the footpads and in the area around the anus and external genitals. Panting cools the body, and the brain is cooled by a complex heat-exchange system involving a network of small blood vessels in a chamber at the base of the brain called the *cavernous sinus*. This keeps the brain from receiving blood that is too warm for its proper functioning, which is especially important during exercise, when the blood temperature can shoot up.

Reproduction There is not much that is unusual in the reproductive

system of cats. Males have permanently scrotal testes and, like other carnivores (except hyenas) male cats have a bone in the penis (the os penis or baculum). This is comparatively smaller than it is in dogs. The tip of the penis (the glans) is covered with backward-directed spines whose function seems to be to provide stimulation for the female so that her eggs are released to coincide with copulation. Cats have

CAT JAW SHOWING CARNASSIAL SHEAR
Shading indicates the shearing facets on an upper premolar and a lower molar. The shearing motion helps cats slice chunks of meat off their prey.

up to six pairs of mammary glands, the number varying with the size of a typical litter.

Tail As well as being a good signal of a cat's mood, the tail seems to be used mainly for balance. In larger, heavier cats, such as the cheetah, the tail may also be helpful when the animal is changing direction during a high-speed chase.

RETRACTIBLE CLAWS

When the claws are retracted (top right), the spring ligament is contracted and the dorsal and ventral muscles are relaxed. This is the normal state of the claws when the cat is at rest. In use (bottom right), the opposite action takes place, with the dorsal and ventral muscles contracting and the spring ligament stretching. The claws are now protruding beyond their sheaths. Among the cats, the cheetah was once thought to have non-retractile claws, but this was a mistake. It merely lacks the sheaths that cover the claws in other cat species.

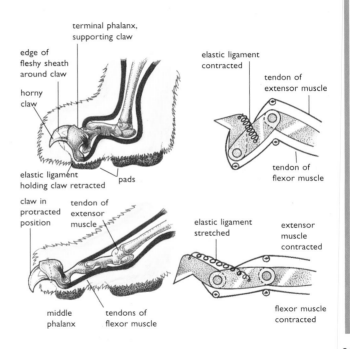

terminal phalanx, supporting claw

edge of fleshy sheath around claw

horny claw

elastic ligament holding claw retracted

pads

elastic ligament contracted

tendon of extensor muscle

tendon of flexor muscle

claw in protracted position

tendon of extensor muscle

elastic ligament stretched

extensor muscle contracted

middle phalanx

tendons of flexor muscle

flexor muscle contracted

CAMOUFLAGE AND FUR

While cat breeds vary only slightly in their morphology, the variety of head and ear shapes, eye shapes and colors, and hair types, colors and patterns is almost endless.

Two Sphynx cats: a brown mackeral tabby and a black.

Cats' bodies range from the short, thick, cobby body of the Persian, Manx and Exotic Shorthair to the long, lean and tubular body of the Siamese and Oriental Shorthair.

In between there are the more moderate body types that strike a balance between the cobbiness of the Persian and the svelteness of the Siamese. They include Burmese, American Shorthair and Havana Brown.

Persian

Hair As a result of cross-breeding, there is now a huge variety of hair lengths and types. Lengths range from the Sphynx, with almost no hair, to the full, thick and flowing coat of the Persian. Between these two extremes are the shorthaired breeds, such as the

Cornish Rex, Burmese, Russian Blue and Siamese, and the medium-haired breeds, such as the Somali, Abyssinian and Balinese. Some cats have double coats, such as the Manx, Somali and Russian Blue, while others should be fine, silky and close lying, as in the Burmese, Siamese, Oriental and Bombay.

There are hundreds of color combinations with some hair colors having a different texture. White hair, for example, is normally soft and silky, blue hair is cottony and dense, and black hair is usually harsher and with a thicker texture, as are the ticked and tabby hairs.

The hair on some cats is actually one of their more distinctive features: the Selkirk Rex looks like a woolly sheep; the Devon Rex has loose, soft waves; and the Cornish Rex has short, tight waves. Other coats, such as those of the Russian Blue and Exotic Shorthair, are so dense and plush that running your fingers through them is a delight.

Basic colors Blue-eyed white, Copper-eyed white, Odd-eyed white, Black (ebony), Cream, Blue, Red, Chocolate, Lilac (lavender).

Other colors Golden, Cameo, Brown, Silver, Fawn, Cinnamon.

Colorpoints Lilac point, Chocolate point, Blue point, Seal point, Red point, Tortie point, Lynx point, Torbie point.

Tabby colors Cream, Brown, Blue, Red, Chocolate, Lilac, Silver, Cameo, Golden.

Tabby patterns Classic, Mackerel, Spotted, Ticked (agouti).

Chocolate Ocicat

Tortoiseshell Red and black (basic), Blue cream, Lilac cream, Chocolate cream.

Particolor Calico (red, black and white), Chocolate calico (red, chocolate and white), Blue calico (red, blue and white), Lilac calico (red, lilac and white), Bicolor (white with any basic color or white with tabby color), Van (white with a smaller area than the bicolor of any basic color, mainly on head, tail and legs), Calico Van (white with a small area of any two basic colors, mainly on head, tail and legs).

Torbie Tabby colors, Tortoiseshell colors, Tabby with white, Torbie with white (can also come in colorpoints and white).

Shaded coats are Chinchilla, Shaded, Smoke. Chinchilla, Shaded and Smoke tipping can be added to Basic solid colors, Bicolors, Golden, Calico, Cameo, Tabby, Torbie, Tortoiseshell and Van.

HEADS AND EARS

Like us, your cat uses facial expressions to communicate at close range. While his ears are busy picking all kinds of interesting information, they are, at the same time, also sending messages about his mood and level of anxiety.

Heads The shape of domestic cats' heads can be divided into three basic types—wedge-shaped (or triangular), round and rectangular. Siamese and Oriental Short-hairs are just two examples of breeds with

*Tabby Bengal:
modified wedge*

wedge-shaped heads. Breeds such as the Abyssinian and Turkish Angora have a modified wedge, which is still triangular in shape but instead of sharp angles, it is gently curved or rounded.

A round head is found in breeds such as the Persian, Exotic Shorthair and British Shorthair. A modified round head (one that is not quite so round) is desirable in such breeds as the Burmese, Manx and American Shorthair.

A rectangular head is broad across the eyes and tapers down to a

slightly narrower muzzle, giving the overall look of a rectangle. Both the Maine Coon and Havana Brown fall into this category.

Ears The size, shape and placement of a cat's ears differ widely from breed to breed. They range from small to large, wide to narrow at the base, set high to low on the head, with pointed to rounded tips. There are the small, forward-folded ears of the Scottish Fold and the folded-back ears of the American Curl.

Other small ears include those of the Persian and Exotic Shorthair, which are set far apart, almost to the sides of the head. Medium-sized ears set moderately far apart are found on the Burmese and British Shorthair, while tall, almost bat-like ears that are strikingly large, set close together and bolt upright

Oriental blue: wedge-shaped head

belong to the Cornish Rex. The ears of the Devon Rex are very wide at the base, and are set so far apart and low down on the sides of the head that the cat looks quite elfin. The distinctive triangular ears of the Siamese and Oriental Shorthair are set almost to flare out and continue the triangular lines of the head.

Hearing The fine muscular control cats have over the outer part of the ear increases their ability to locate the source of tiny sounds from any direction. This helps them to locate potential small prey. We do not

Persian calico: round head

know how the hearing range and sensitivity of the larger cats compares with small domestic cats or humans.

While cats have excellent hearing when young, it seems to start to deteriorate by the time they are about five years old.

Ear signals During a feline encounter, the position of your cat's ears sends clear signals to the other cat. At first they will stand straight up and forward because he is alert. If he perceives a threat, the ears move down and sideways in direct relationship to the intensity of the threat. If he is frightened, they will be pulled right down to the side.

Norwegian blue and white: rectangular head

EYES

All felids have large eyes for their skull size, but those of nocturnal species are especially large for maximum light-gathering ability. The eyes of domestic cats are almost as large as human eyes, and they can open their pupils far wider than we can.

Stereoscopic view At birth, kittens are blind, with eyes tightly closed. They remain so for about a week or 10 days, and the vision is poor for the first few months. All cats have large, forward-facing eyes that allow the visual fields to overlap substantially. This means that they have stereoscopic perception in most of their visual field.

This arrangement works well for predators, especially those that stalk or ambush their victims, because such hunters must pick up the slightest movement made by

Balinese: vivid blue almond-shaped eyes

potential prey before they are themselves spotted. Stereoscopic vision allows the cats to judge position and distance accurately, which is vital for hunters.

Most important sense Cats rely heavily on sight and have excellent night vision and a wide visual field. The pupils are able to dilate fully to a circle in low-light conditions, but in bright sunshine they contract to vertical slits to protect the highly sensitive retina.

Glow-in-the-dark eyes One attribute of a cat's eyes heightens their sensitivity to light, but limits their acuity. This is a layer of reflective cells, called the *tapetum lucidum*, found in many nocturnal animals and almost all carnivores. It functions by reflecting the light back through the sensory cells to double the effect of each photon of light. While this makes the eyes more sensitive, the reflected image is not perfect and appears blurred. The *tapetum lucidum* is what makes eyes caught in headlights seem to glow.

Siberian: almond-shaped eyes

Scottish Fold: round eyes

Siamese: slanted eyes

Shape Although all eyes are round, some cats' eyes appear to have a different shape because of the eye opening, or aperture. There are only three basic shapes—round, almond (or oval) and slanted.

Domestic cats with round eyes include the Burmese, Exotic Shorthair and Persian. Cats with almond-shaped eyes include the Abyssinian and American Shorthair. Cats with slanted eyes include the Siamese and Oriental Shorthair.

If you are planning to breed or show your pedigreed cat, eye color must conform to the coat color in all breeds, except those permitted to have any eye color, such as the Manx, Scottish Fold and the Rexes, to mention only a few.

Most other breeds must have the correct eye color for their color class (see the specifications in A Guide to Breeds, starting on p. 202).

Sometimes a cat's eyes will be two different colors, but this has no effect on the animal's sight. In white cats with blue eyes, the sight is normal but there is sometimes an ear defect that causes deafness.

Third eyelid Like most other vertebrates, the cat has a third eyelid called the nictitating membrane. Its appearance is a good indicator of the cat's health (if you can see it, your cat is not well). It looks like pale, whitish tissue and lies in the inside corner of the eye.

Each time the cat blinks, the eyelids clean the surface of the eye. The inside surface of each lid and the visible part of the eye are covered with a membrane that is kept moist by tears released through pinhole ducts in the corner of the eye.

TAILS

There is no really good functional explanation for a cat tail, although it may help cats to balance. In fact, some species have dispensed with their tails almost completely.

Persian

57 varieties

Cat tails come in many different sizes and shapes, from the short thick tail of the Persian to the tailless Manx. While the Japanese Bobtail has a tail that resembles a pompom and extends out from the body no further than a couple of inches (5 cm), the Cornish Rex, Siamese and Oriental have long, slender and almost whip-like tails.

Other long tails, but not as slender, can be found in the Turkish Angora, Maine Coon, Ragdoll and Russian Blue. Other breeds, such as the Burmese, Exotic, American Shorthair and British Shorthair, have medium-length tails.

Markings Tail markings of most cat species include rings and tips in a contrasting color. These may serve to make tail signals more obvious. In aggressive encounters, a cat swishes its tail from side to side as a threat. The contrasting markings may be meant to catch the eye of the other

Japanese Bobtail

British Shorthair

both in fights and trying to flee from a confrontation, as well as car accidents. Fortunately, a badly injured tail can be amputated with no real harm to the cat, although he might look and feel a bit odd and take a while to get used to his new body shape.

Never pull a cat's tail, because you can damage the spinal cord, which runs through inside the spinal column. If there are children living in the house or coming to visit, make sure they are shown how to hold a cat properly (see p. 72), and that they not pull your cat's tail or otherwise mistreat it.

Tailless breeds This best-known tailless breed in the Manx, although many cats of this breed do have some vestiges of a tail. Taillessness comes from a spinal defect, and it is important not to breed two completely tailless Manx cats.

Siamese

protagonist and make the threat more emphatic and noticeable.

Injuries Tails seem particularly vulnerable to injury. Common accidents involve tails being caught in house or car doors, bites acquired

CATS IN THE WILD

Among the carnivores, the cats are perhaps the most impressively adapted for a predatory lifestyle—streamlined runners or stealthy ambush hunters, with razor claws and lethal teeth. For all their diversity of color, size and habits, the felids (or true cats) are remarkably uniform in body and skull shape and general proportions, especially in their dentition. Although their teeth are not designed for chewing, their long canine teeth are typical of meat eaters. The success of the felids is partly due to how generalized they are in many of their features, but they also retain many useful primitive characteristics from the earliest ancestors of the entire order Carnivora.

LIONS

Among the largest and most powerful of the cat family, lions have developed effective strategies for survival. They are the only cats that regularly work together to make a kill and share the spoils more or less democratically. Communal living makes it easier to defend whatever territory they need to occupy.

The sociable lion (*Panthera leo*) lives in prides of varying numbers, the females of which are usually related. Up to 40 animals may belong to the group but more often 12–15 live and hunt together in a well-delineated territory that is patrolled and kept marked by the dominant males. Young males, pushed out of their family group when their father loses control of the pride, may form small groups for mutual protection and help in hunting activities until they are able to establish themselves in a pride.

When a dominant male begins to lose his edge, because of age, loss of

A typical pride consists of several generations of a dozen or more related animals.

teeth, or injury, younger, stronger males are quick to seize the chance to oust him. The new dominant male kills or chases away juveniles and cubs. Females immediately come into season and he repeatedly mates with as many of them as possible to ensure the survival of his genes.

Cubs are born, usually to several females about the same time, some six months later. Females cooperate in rearing litters of one to four cubs, readily suckling the offspring of other females and adopting any youngsters that become orphaned.

Range Lions once roamed extensive areas of central southern Europe, India and northern Africa. They are now found only in the west of India and the semidesert and upland areas of Africa. Their preferred habitats are savannahs, grassy plains, arid woodlands and semideserts, where the browns and ochers of their coats help them to blend in with the colors of the surrounding landscape.

Diet Like most carnivores, lions work hard for their food, often teaming up to stalk and bring down the large animals, such as zebras and antelopes, which are their usual prey. They also take giraffe and smaller animals, and will eat carrion. Often it

is the lionesses who make the kill, but when it comes to eating, males take precedence over females and younger animals. An old male who has lost his place in the pride has a poor chance of surviving for very long, and will probably not live beyond 12 years of age.

Two related females share a meal. Juveniles must wait their turn. Animals from a different pride are not welcome at the feast.

Male and female lions: the brown mane of the male becomes fuller and darker with age.

TIGERS

With his distinctive striped coat, the magnificent *Panthera tigris* is easily recognized. A formidable predator, and the largest of the living cats, his dark brown or black vertical stripes afford him instant camouflage in the low-light conditions in which he hunts, often between dusk and dawn.

The tiger is the only felid with stripes, so is probably the most easily recognized big cat. Its coat varies from dark orange to reddish ocher, with creamy white on the belly, neck and insides of the limbs. Dark stripes run vertically across the body.

Litters of two or three are suckled by the mother for about six months, but they remain with her, learning the skills of hunting, until the next litter is born, perhaps when the juveniles are about two years old. Neighboring females may have territories that are exclusive or overlapping, while a male's home range may take in that of several breeding females.

Range Tigers live in a variety of habitats, from the snow-clad taiga to tropical forests, as long as there is a plentiful supply of game and a reliable source of fresh drinking water year-round. Once a female has established her home range, she usually stays there for life, or until forced out by one of her daughters. Tigers are found in India, Nepal, Bhutan, Bangladesh, Burma, Thailand, Vietnam, the USSR, and perhaps China.

Diet Although tigers hunt alone, a kill may be shared by several adults. Prey consists of whatever unwary or vulnerable creature happens to stray across their path, but most often they attack deer, pigs and even buffalo. Some tigers seem to have favored ambush spots, especially near drinking places where potential prey may be distracted or off-guard. They readily kill domestic livestock and will also kill humans.

Tigers prefer to live near fresh water and they are strong and fearless swimmers.

White tigers (below) are not a separate subspecies, nor are they albinos; their coat coloration is the result of a recessive gene. Occasionally, all-black tigers also occur.

LEOPARDS

Cautious, tough and pragmatic, the adaptable leopard is able to live in the shadow of humans more effectively than any of the other big cats. It solves the problem of competition by hunting at different times of day to its larger cousins.

Range Among the most adaptable of the large cats, the leopard survives throughout much of Africa, except

The leopard (*Panthera pardus*) is quite similar in appearance to the jaguar, but it lacks the jaguar's massive head and robust physique. Its fur varies from gray to rusty brown, with desert and savannah populations generally being paler. The coat is covered with small black spots and rosettes, with no spots inside the rosettes. All-black (melanistic) leopards are common, especially in tropical forests.

Two or three young are born in a secluded den after a gestation period of 90–105 days. They remain with their mother until they are from 15–24 months old.

the Sahara, as well as in parts of Israel, the Middle East, Pakistan, India, Southeast Asia, China and Siberia. It lives in a variety of habitats, wherever there is enough food and cover for hunting.

Diet Leopards are stealthy and solitary hunters, sometimes stalking prey over very long distances. While females appear to respect the boundaries

Individual animals can be identified by the number and position of spots on the muzzle.

Black coats provide good camouflage for leopards commonly found in tropical forests.

of each other's territories, males may roam over the home ranges of several females. Leopards often eat the limbs and entrails of their kill as the first meal and hide the remainder for later. They either drag the carcass to thick cover or lodge it in the relative safety of a tree fork, where it is well out of range of hyenas and even airborne scavengers such as vultures.

Common prey are large ungulates (gazelle, deer, pig), and monkeys, but they will also eat rodents and insects.

Unlike tigers and jaguars, leopards don't need a constant supply of drinking water, but can survive on the moisture they get from the bodies of their victims. However, where water is readily available, they will drink regularly.

JAGUARS

The third-largest of the big cats, after the tiger and the lion, today's jaguar is much smaller than its giant ancestor, which once roamed freely throughout the North American continent. Although they often rest in trees, these elusive animals are thought to hunt mainly on the ground.

The jaguar (*Panthera onca*) is a powerful, deep-chested, stocky cat with a large rounded head and short, stocky limbs. Its size and spotted coat make it look like a heavyset leopard, but there are minor differences in the spot patterns of the two animals. The jaguar's short fur varies from pale gold to a rich rusty red, and is patterned with a series of dark rosettes that enclose one or two smaller spots. Along the middle of its back, a row of black spots sometimes merges into a solid line. All-black animals are not uncommon.

One to four young are born after a gestation period of 93–105 days.

All-black (melanistic) jaguars are fairly common. The characteristic spots show through the darker background of the fur.

They remain with the mother for about two years before establishing their own territory. The territories of more than one female may overlap and a male's territory may overlap that of several females.

Range Jaguars frequent well-watered areas, such as the swampy grasslands of the Brazilian Pantanal. In other areas they often use forest growing alongside streams, rivers or lakes. They enter water with no hesitation and are strong swimmers. They are found from the south of central Mexico, through Central America, and into South America as far south as northern Argentina.

Diet Being good climbers, jaguars often rest in trees, but they are thought to hunt mainly on the ground. These powerful solitary hunters will feed on almost anything that's available, including lizards, snakes, capybara, caiman, small mammals, deer, fish, turtles and cattle. The jaguar's strong jaws and robust canine teeth enable it to kill livestock weighing three or four times its own weight, often with a lethal bite to the back of the skull rather than seizing the neck or throat as many other large cats do.

SNOW LEOPARDS

The subject of myth and folklore for many centuries, these magnificent, secretive animals are rarely seen, even by enterprising mountain people. They are superbly adapted to the rigors of their preferred remote and rugged habitat.

The snow leopard (*Panthera uncia*) is an exotic-looking animal with gray-green eyes and long, thick, smoke-gray fur patterned with large, dark rosettes and spots. The head is small with a high forehead, and the ears are short and rounded. The legs are comparatively short, with large, broad paws.

Range Snow leopards are found in remote, steep, rugged terrain at high altitudes, and have been recorded in alpine meadows, alpine steppe scrub, and high-altitude forests. They usually live above the tree line at elevations of 8,900–19,700 feet (2,700–6,000 meters), but descend sometimes to lower areas in search of food during winter.

These mainly solitary animals are widely distributed in mountainous regions of Central Asia as well as parts of the USSR, Mongolia, China,

Nepal, Bhutan, India, Pakistan and possibly Afghanistan. Their secretive habits, low numbers and sparse distribution, along with difficult field conditions, have long hindered attempts to study them, so little is known of their habits. The territory of a male may overlap that of one or more females.

Diet The snow leopard hunts mainly around dawn, dusk, or through the night. It preys mainly on wild sheep and marmots, although it is also known to feed on musk deer, ibex, markhor, pika, hares and birds, and to eat willow twigs and other vegetation. There are records of it killing domestic sheep and goats, and after such forays it is often hunted and killed itself, in spite of the protected status it holds in most countries. There are no records of it killing people.

The snow leopard

PUMAS

The puma has the most extensive range of any terrestrial animal in the Western hemisphere, but it is known by different names in the various regions it inhabits. The mountain lion, American lion, cougar, panther, painter and catamount (cat on a mountain) are all names given to the puma, so the confusion over its "proper" name is likely to continue.

A cub with spotted coat and bright blue eyes.

The puma (*Felis concolor*) has small ears, a long neck, a slim, elongated body, and a long tail. It is one of only two plain-colored big cats (the other being the lion). Males do not have manes, and the coat can be almost any shade from red-brown to blue-gray. The reddish colors seem to predominate in tropical areas while the gray tones are more common in northern regions. Puma

mother, but adults are basically solitary animals.

Range These animals are found in coniferous forests, tropical forests, swamps, grasslands and brush country, from sea level to 14,765 feet (4,500 meters) through Canada, North America (west of the great plains), southern Florida, Mexico, Central and South America.

Females may share overlapping territories, and males may overlap the range of one or more females, but there is usually little overlap between resident males.

Diet In general, deer are the main part of the puma's diet. Other prey include beavers, porcupines, hares, raccoons, opossums and feral hogs. The kill is often dragged to a secluded spot and, after the cat has eaten its fill, it may cover the carcass with vegetation. Large prey, such as an elk, can provide enough food for a week or more.

cubs are born with a spotted coat, but the spots fade and disappear as the young mature.

There are usually two or three cubs in a litter and the gestation period is 90–95 days. Cubs start to eat meat when about six weeks old, but continue to suckle until about three months or more. They are fully grown and independent at about two years. Littermates may stay together for a few months after leaving their

43

CHEETAHS

Noted for its beauty and speed, the magnificent cheetah is now classified as endangered, mainly because the spread of agriculture is causing its habitat to shrink. Cub mortality in the wild has always been high, most being lost to predators.

The cheetah (*Acinonyx jubatus*) has a slender muscular body and long powerful legs that combine to make it the world's fastest land mammal. The head is small, with a short muzzle, wide nostrils, high-set eyes, and small rounded ears. The short, coarse fur is tawny yellow, marked with round black spots. The tail is long. Even when retracted, the claws are exposed, which gives this cat added traction for turning and maneuvering, and during acceleration.

Females live alone with their cubs but are not territorial. The home ranges of females are large, and several may overlap, but females tend to avoid each other. As many as eight cubs, but more usually three to five, are born after a gestation period of 90–95 days.

The cubs lose their distinctive gray natal coat at about four months, are weaned by about six months, and leave their mother at between 13 and 20 months. Siblings usually remain together for several months more.

Male siblings may remain together even longer, forming small coalitions of up to four, which gives them both mutual protection and a great advantage in hunting. They are able to take larger prey than they could manage alone, and share their kill.

Cheetahs can run for short bursts at 65–70 miles per hour (110kph). The sequence below illustrates the rotary gallop of a sprinting cheetah. The hind legs land first on alternate sides, and this is followed by a phase of floating, when no feet are on the ground. The forelimbs then land on alternate sides, followed by a period of crossed flight with all feet gathered up under the body.

Range The cheetah's style of hunting works best in open areas where there is enough cover to conceal it from potential prey. It is found in open grasslands, semidesert and thick bush throughout Africa and the Middle East.

Diet Cheetahs hunt by daylight, often in the late morning and early evening when competition is less keen. They take animals such as gazelles, impalas, wildebeest calves and hares, stalking their quarry until close enough to make a sudden dash and then pursuing them in a short and dramatic high-speed chase.

LYNXES

Bobcat (Lynx rufus)

Of the five species within the genus *Lynx*, the bobcat has been the most successful in adapting to changing habitat conditions. All are members of the Pantherine family and have prominent ears tipped with tufts of black hair.

Caracal (Lynx caracal)

The caracal is a slender, long-legged, reddish-brown cat found through northern, central and southern Africa, as well as in parts of the Middle East, Saudi Arabia, the USSR, Afghanistan, Pakistan and northwest and central India. It prefers dry woodlands, arid hilly steppe, acacia scrub, savannah and dry mountainous areas, where it lives mainly on birds, rodents and mammals, hunting at night and sometimes taking quite large prey. It is about the size of a springer spaniel and has short, straight, unspotted fur.

Bobcats are very similar in appearance to other species of lynx, but generally have shorter legs and smaller feet. Their short, soft, dense fur comes in a variety of colors from light gray to reddish-brown. The coat may be marked with black or dark brown spots or bars, and the backs of the ears are black with a prominent white spot. The short tail is white underneath with a broad black band on the upper tip and several indistinct dark bands. These solitary animals are found in widely differing habitats from southern Canada to Central Mexico, though numbers are small. Rabbits and hares are their preferred diet, but they also prey on rodents, birds, snakes and small deer.

North American lynx (Lynx canadensis)

The North American lynx is usually yellowish-brown, sometimes patterned with dark spots. It has a short tail, with several dark rings and a dark tip. The feet are large and densely furred. It ranges through wooded areas of Canada and Alaska, feeding almost exclusively on snowshoe hares, but will also scavenge, or take other small mammals, birds and caribou calves.

The Eurasian lynx is nearly twice as large as the North American and its dark spots are usually well defined. It roams over forested areas of western Europe, the USSR, Scandinavia, Asia Minor, Iran, Iraq, Mongolia, Manchuria and parts of Soviet Central Asia. Rabbits and hares are a major component of its diet, supplemented with rodents and birds.

The Spanish lynx is much more heavily spotted than the others. It inhabits the remote mountainous regions of south-western Spain and parts of Portugal, hunting rabbit, ducks and fallow deer fawns.

Eurasian lynx (Lynx lynx)

Spanish lynx (Lynx pardinus)

SERVALS AND OCELOTS

These two medium-sized cats have very different evolutionary histories but, although they live on different continents, both make their living catching essentially the same kind of food—small rodents. The serval patrols grasslands, while the ocelot is more of a forest hunter.

Serval (Felis serval)

Servals This tall, long-legged cat has a small, slim head dominated by a pair of very large ears. The short tail reaches only to the hocks. The coat is a tawny gold marked with rounded black dots that vary in size from a freckle to one inch (2.5 cm).

One to three kittens are born after a gestation period of about 74 days in a well-camouflaged den or abandoned burrow dug by another animal. The young start to eat solid food when they are about a month old. They remain with their mother for about one year.

Range The serval prefers well-watered grasslands and never strays far from water. It is distributed widely through Africa and is quite abundant in areas south of the Sahara, although it has not been sighted for more than 25 years in the Atlas region of North Africa, where it

Ocelot (Felis pardalis)

was formerly common. The ranges of breeding females do not overlap, but a male's domain may overlap that of several females. Territories are maintained by frequent marking.

Diet A highly specialized rodent catcher, this animal is almost exclusively a ground hunter. It uses its large ears and excellent hearing to locate prey in the tall grass. Although rodents are the preferred food, it will also eat frogs, lizards, mole rats, small birds and insects.

Ocelots have short, close fur marked with both solid and open dark spots that sometimes run in lines along the body. The tail is ringed with black or has black bars on the upper surface. The coat pattern is very similar to that of the margay, but ocelots are generally larger, have shorter tails and slightly smaller eyes. The ears are rounded with a prominent white spot on the back.

One or sometimes two kittens are born after a gestation of about 79–82 days. They remain with their mother for about two years.

Range These mainly solitary animals are found in a broad range of tropical and subtropical habitats, including evergreen and deciduous forests, dry scrub, and seasonally flooded savannahs, from southern Texas, parts of Mexico and Central America down into South America to Argentina. Their range is shrinking, however, because of habitat destruction.

The territories of breeding females do not overlap, but a male's range may overlap that of several females.

Diet Largely nocturnal these predators hunt in dense cover. Prey comprises chiefly rodents and other small mammals, but they sometimes take animals as large as an agouti, or catch birds, fish, snakes, lizards and land crabs.

Ocelot (Felis pardalis)

OTHER WILD CATS

Of the 37 species of cat found throughout the world, we are familiar with only about seven of the larger ones. These have been studied both in the wild and in zoos and have been bred successfully in captivity. If we are to preserve the less well known species, we must learn more about their needs and life cycles.

Kodkod

The kodkod (*Felis guigna*) About the size of a small domestic cat, the kodkod is one of the smallest cats in the Western hemisphere. It is found in a restricted area of Chile and Argentina in coniferous forests, wooded areas and semi-open habitats. Its favored habitats are under threat from logging and agricultural expansion, so its future is uncertain.

The kodkod's fur is sometimes black, or buff, or gray-brown, and is heavily marked with small round spots. These sometimes merge into streaks on the shoulders. The tail is marked with a series of black rings. All-black (melanistic) kodkods are quite common.

Not much is known about this rare creature, but it is probably a solitary hunter, feeding on small mammals and birds in the wild.

Pallas' cat (*Felis manul*) is a heavy, fluffy-looking animal with short, stout legs. Its dense, long, grayish or reddish fur is twice as long on the underbody as it is on the back and sides, providing insulation against the cold, snowy winters that are common throughout most of its range. It is found from the Caspian Sea and Iran to southeastern Siberia and China. It is thought to hunt mainly by sight, eating small mammals, hares and birds.

The oncilla (*Felis tigrina*) is even smaller than the kodkod. It has thick, soft fur marked with black or brown spots and rosettes, ideal camouflage for its forest habitat. It is found in cloud forest and humid lowland forest from sea level to

Oncilla

3,280 feet (1,000 meters) in Central and South America, from Costa Rica south to northern Argentina. Rare in most parts of its range, it is probably becoming rarer as its habitat shrinks with logging and to make way for coffee plantations.

Little is known of the oncilla's habits, but in captivity one or two kittens are born after a gestation period of 74–76 days. It is thought to be a solitary nocturnal animal, like most cats, hunting on the ground for rodents and small birds.

OTHER WILD CATS continued

Clouded leopard of Asia

The jaguarundi (*Felis yagouaroundi*) has a long, low-slung, slender body, short legs, and a very long tail. Its head is small and flattened, and the ears are small and rounded. Overall, it looks more like a weasel or otter than a cat. One of the few unspotted cats, it has red-brown or gray fur of an almost uniform color. It lives in a

Jaguarundi

The clouded leopard of Asia (*Neofelis nebulosa*) has a most unusual coat, patterned with large, dark, cloud-shaped markings that become darker toward the rear. The lower parts of the legs, head, shoulders and belly are covered with large dark spots. The legs are short and powerful and the tail very long. Rarely seen in the wild, there is some controversy as to whether the clouded leopard is an arboreal species or a terrestrial hunter that makes use of logging roads in logged forests. It is found in the Himalayas, southern China, Taiwan, Malaysia, Sumatra and Borneo. It is thought to feed on birds, monkeys, pigs, cattle, goats, deer and porcupines.

variety of habitats from arid thorn forests to dense second-growth forests and swampy grasslands. It seems more able to live in open areas than most other neotropical cats. A strong swimmer, it is also found in riverine habitats.

The jaguarundi occurs from southern Texas through Mexico, Central and South America east of the Andes to northern Argentina. Hunting mainly by day on the ground, it preys on birds, arthropods, small mammals and armadillos, and it eats fruit.

The margay (*Felis wiedii*) has soft, thick fur marked with dark brown or black streaks or spots with paler, open centers. Its coat is very similar to both the larger ocelot and the smaller oncilla, but the margay's head is shorter and more rounded, its eyes are larger and its tail is longer than either. It is always found in arboreal habitats, usually humid tropical forests from Mexico through Central and South America east of the Andes to Argentina. It hunts at night, mostly in the trees but also on the ground, preying on rodents, birds, reptiles and insects.

Although widespread, its numbers are probably not great and little is known about its social life, although it is probably solitary. Margays in captivity give birth to single young after an 81-day gestation period. The young start to eat solid food at about two months and are fully grown at about 10 months.

Margay

FERAL CATS

Despite its closeness to humans since the wild cat was first domesticated, probably in Egypt about 4,000 years ago, the ways cats behave are not yet fully understood. When domestic cats go feral, their behavior bears little resemblance to that of your mild-mannered cat on the couch.

Most close relatives of the domestic cat live in habitats where food is scarce for at least part of the year. They adopt a mostly solitary lifestyle, and occupy large, exclusive, ranges, which they defend ferociously.

Lost or abandoned domestic cats can quickly become feral, even in the urban environment. They may become so wary of people that they are difficult to reclaim or rehabilitate.

Life in the wild When domestic cats go feral, they are well able to survive, but their predations wreak havoc on local populations of small native animals and birds. This puts feral cats very much in the bad books of conservationists, who rightly see them as a major pest.

Reproduction Feral cats can bear several litters a year and, not being socialized with people early in life, the young grow into adults that are virtually impossible to catch and handle without physical or chemical restraint. Their illnesses go untreated and these cats can become reservoirs for parasites and infectious diseases. Population pressure means fierce competition, so fighting is prevalent and infections are quickly passed on. Diseases such as the feline immuno-deficiency virus (FIV/ AIDS) now occur at a higher rate in feral animals than in the general cat population.

Fighting Feral cats inflict hideous injuries on one another in their territorial wars. Where their ranges overlap those of domestic pets, the ferals usually come off best in a fight. Common injuries include corneal scratches, but the greatest danger is the introduction and spread of disease. Bite wounds always become infected, so abscesses are rife.

Rehabilitation of feral cats is, at best, usually only partly successful, especially if the early socialization period with humans was missed, as in second-generation ferals. Although they may come to accept offerings of food, they will never become tame.

Feral cats are well able to survive in the wild, but they create a big problem for native animals. Expert hunters, their predations can rapidly wipe out endangered species of small mammals and birds.

PART TWO

CATS AS PETS

CATS AS PETS

YOU AND YOUR CAT

Once considered demigods, cats have been important members of the household for thousands of years. Today, millions of proud owners around the world enjoy the unconditional love and friendship bestowed upon them by their cat. Theirs is an unassailable bond that can last a lifetime. Having a cat can do wonders for a person's health and happiness. But owning a cat is a significant responsibility and every potential owner needs to bear in mind that it takes time and effort to make our pets' lives as happy as possible right from the moment we choose them and bring them home. That effort will be rewarded though, with years of companionship and love.

CHOOSING A CAT

**Are you looking for a buddy or a companion cat?
Or are you interested in breeding and showing cats?
Only a very small percentage of cat owners want to
breed and exhibit their cats. Most are looking for
that special cat to share their heart and home.**

STARTING OUT
A new kitten is the beginning of a
wonderful friendship. Just be certain that
you and your family can afford the time
and money to care for him properly.

Before you acquire a cat, ask yourself
if you are willing and able to provide
for him for some 18 years or more.
Do you have a safe environment in
which he can live? Do you have the
time to groom and care for him?
Are your children trained in the
responsibilities of pet ownership?
Are your other pets willing to accept
a newcomer?

If you answer yes to these
questions, then ask yourself if you
can afford a cat. The initial cost of
acquiring a kitten or cat is nothing
compared with the ongoing costs of
keeping him safe and healthy. You

need to be sure you can
afford to feed him, as
well as keep him current
on his inoculations,
yearly physicals and any other
veterinary care he may need.

If you are still answering yes, you
should know that the time and
money you spend will be repaid
more than a thousand times over by
the companionship and love he will
give you.

It doesn't matter how large or
small your house is—cats fit in
anywhere, so any type of home will
do. Many pet-owners living in cities

are apartment dwellers, but the
absence of a yard is not a problem.
All cats can adapt to life indoors.
Even if they object at first, simply
ignore their pleas to go outside and
they will eventually quieten down. If
you live in an area where your cat is

safe outdoors, then any yard is big enough for his needs.

Kitten or adult? There are many adult cats that, for various reasons, need to find loving homes. It's not easy adopting an adult, but the gratitude and affection you reap will be well worth your patience. Kittens, on the other hand, are easier to adopt as they adapt more readily. If you have other cats in your home, it is best to bring in a kitten, whereas if you have no other cats, you may want to adopt a fully grown cat. An adult is not as boisterous as a kitten, and so may be more suitable for an older person.

Cats for children Cats and children mix very well with a little help from you. Although a kitten may have a hard time escaping the tail-pulling and hair-yanking inflicted by a toddler, an older cat will simply move away if playtime turns into wartime. And most cats are quite

forgiving of children and will tolerate being held in all sorts of undignified positions. Let an adult try to hold him with his head dangling down and he will react with outrage, but a child can carry him any which way and he may tolerate it.

If you are bringing a kitten into a house with children, encourage the children to stay away from the kitten until he approaches them. And make sure there is proper supervision until you are confident they are mixing together safely.

A lap-cat Not every cat will sit on your lap. Some are too busy or too highly strung to settle down for long. Others with thick or long coats, just don't like the added warmth of our laps. They move away because they are feeling uncomfortably warm. Since all cats are lap-size, if you really want to increase your chances of him being a lap-cat, one of the shorthaired breeds is for you, but there are no guarantees.

MAKING FRIENDS
Although they may not warm to each other immediately, give your pets time to get to know each other, and after a little while they should be the best of friends.

LONGHAIR OR SHORTHAIR?

The main consideration governing your choice of breed is which appeals most, but commonsense dictates that the coat should suit the climate and living conditions. Keep in mind that with longhaired breeds you are looking at a big commitment in time to keep your cat groomed to perfection.

EASY-CARE COAT
If you don't wish to be committed to extensive grooming time, perhaps one of the shorthaired breeds is best for you.

Choosing a breed There are many considerations to take into account when choosing a breed. Those Persian cats with baby-doll faces and long flowing coats may appeal to you, but do you have the time and the inclination to groom them each and every day?

A day without combing this kind of coat is an invitation to tangles and matting. A happy compromise enabling you to have that doll-like Persian face coupled with a short coat that requires less grooming is the Exotic Shorthair. In the United Kingdom, a similar type of cat is called the British Shorthair, and in mainland Europe it is called the European Shorthair.

Are you a person who likes peace and quiet? Then perhaps neither the Siamese nor the Oriental Shorthair is for you because their voices can be very loud. And if you want your curios to remain on their shelves or the coffee table, most of the short-haired breeds are taboo. They just love to rearrange anything movable.

Are there other cats or dogs in the house? Will your new cat have plenty of human companionship, or will he be alone for much of the day? Some breeds cope better than others with being home alone.

Climate Do you live in a place that's hot and humid? If so, a longhaired breed will not be comfortable unless you have air-

BEAUTY SPOT
A Persian such as this likes nothing better than to drape himself in a prominent spot and hang around being admired.

like in his responses to you. Your best bet in selecting your ideal cat is simply to pick one that you like the look of, keeping in mind any special grooming he may require, and then gradually integrate him into your household routine.

Once you decide on a breed you must choose a color, and here the range is truly staggering. A Guide to Breeds (starting on p. 202) will help you decide which cat best suits you, your lifestyle and your family needs.

conditioning. A shorthaired cat will shiver his days away in a cold and windy climate, unless kept strictly indoors. Even then, he will want the furnace going because he doesn't have a thick coat to keep him warm.

Certain breeds, such as the Sphynx (see p. 268) and Rexes (see pp. 232–235), have little or no hair and need special handling. The Sphynx can be easily sunburned, too, so must be sheltered from sunlight.

Indoor or outdoor An indoor/outdoor cat will be more independent because he will retain his wild instincts for survival. A completely indoor cat will surprise you by shedding his independent nature and becoming almost dog-

ACROBAT
An Oriental Shorthair such as this will be active, playful and loving, but they love company and may fret if left alone much.

You and Your Cat

PEDIGREE OR NON-PEDIGREE?

You may have a friend with an adored Siamese, or perhaps you have fallen under the spell of a particular breed at a cat show. If you want a certain appearance or temperament, you're certain to find a breed that has what you want. Just remember that mixed-breed cats can be just as lovable.

IRRESISTIBLE
Blue-eyed Persian kittens would steal anyone's heart, but before you get carried away, ask yourself if you have the time to look after them properly.

Pedigreed cats The main advantage of acquiring a pedigreed cat is that he will be more likely to live up to the breed characteristics and quirks you desire. While all cats are individuals, appearance remains constant within each breed, although some come in so many colors and coat patterns that it is hard to choose. Certain personality traits can also be expected in specific breeds. Some breeds, such as Burmese, Siamese and Abyssinians, are well known for their almost dog-like traits. They love to play and follow their owners around. Others, such as Russian Blues are known to be extremely affectionate as well as being beautiful to look at.

A purebred may appeal to you because of its color, coat, or body shape and, if this is important to you, then choose a pedigreed cat of this breed.

Non-pedigree cats There are far more mixed-breed cats in the world than purebreds. And Mother Nature often paints them more beautifully than many of the pedigreed cats. These less highly bred cats are hardier and better able to fend for themselves. They are easier to care for and cost a lot less to purchase and maintain. While their personalities are less predictable, they still make beautiful, responsive pets.

A friend and playmate If you just want a cat as a companion, then any cat, pedigreed or mixed-breed, will fit the bill. A cat doesn't know or care if he has a pedigree. All cats eat like cats, play like cats, and love us like cats, no matter where they came from.

HUMBLE ORIGINS
Mixed-breed cats often make wonderfully good-natured and affectionate pets.

ARISTOCRATS
Not all pedigree cats are time consuming to care for. This elegant Burmese is almost maintenance-free.

WHAT TO LOOK FOR IN A CAT

Now that you have decided you want a cat as a pet and have selected the type of cat you'd love to have, you need to make sure you buy the right cat from the right place. You want a cat that is healthy, happy and responsive.

Check for signs of illness When you choose that special kitten or cat, you want him to be as fit as possible. His ears should be clean and free of mites. His eyes should be clear, with no debris in the corners. His mouth and gums should be a healthy shade of pink. His nose should not be runny. Run your hands gently down his back and across his hips. He should have enough flesh covering him that you don't feel his backbone and hip bones. His coat and the anal area should look clean.

If your cat is a shorthair, his coat should lie flat and not be dull and open; if he is a longhaired cat, it should be full-bodied and not dry. He should not have bad breath and ideally should have no odor. In a kitten, especially, lightly finger his stomach to make sure it is not distended or out of proportion to the rest of his body.

When handling a strange kitten or cat, do not pick him up and dangle him up in the air. This often frightens him and he will react by crying and trying to escape. Hold him firmly, preferably on your lap, to examine him.

Where to buy Kittens and cats are found abandoned and hiding under cars or bushes. Be careful. They could be feral. Cats can be acquired from

THE ONCE OVER
Before purchasing a kitten or cat, be sure to check that he is fit and healthy.

local animal shelters or by contacting cat rescue groups. These sources, however, will not be able to provide you with details of the cat's forebears, or any possible hereditary defects he may have.

Local newspapers and notices on vets' bulletin boards may also list available kittens and cats. A pet store is another source, but do check it out carefully to ensure that the animals are in good health, are kept in sanitary conditions, and that the pet store stands behind its sales in the form of health guarantees.

Purebred cats are also available through private breeders and catteries. They are also offered for sale—or adoption in the case of older, retired breeding cats—at cat shows.

Cat magazines carry listings of breeders and venues of cat shows and are a

good source for locating cats. When buying a cat from a breeder, let your first impression be your guide. If there is a strong odor in the house, or if the cats flee in fright, then you should not purchase a kitten or cat there. Although most cats will hide temporarily when strangers invade their homes, the well-adjusted cat will soon emerge from hiding to

explore the new person. Nothing is more curious than a cat. It's also a good idea to see the parents of the kitten as this will give you some idea of his size and appearance when fully grown.

If the house or the litter pans are not clean, then the chances are high the kitten will not be clean either.

PAPERWORK
Be sure to receive a record of your kitten's inoculations. If you are acquiring a pedigreed cat for breeding you will also need his pedigree and registration certificates.

SETTLING IN

The exciting moment has arrived for both you and your kitten. Be aware that he may be a little frightened when you bring him home. Make sure he feels safe and secure, and provide plenty of human company while he adjusts to his new surroundings.

It is important that you use a carrier to transport your new kitten home as he could easily become frightened by road traffic. Don't try to carry him in your arms—he could either claw his way out and run away or, if you are in the car, he may inadvertently interfere with the gas pedal or brakes. If a proper carrier is not available, buy an inexpensive one of cardboard at most vets or pet stores.

Settling in When you arrive home with your kitten, confine him to a room where he can get his bearings (your bedroom will do) along with a litter pan and food and water dishes. Don't shut him away by himself. Kittens will miss their siblings and cry all night if left alone. Even if you want an indoor/outdoor cat, never put a kitten outdoors until he is ready.

Always leave a litter pan in the room as you can't expect him to be brave enough to explore a new and strange house for the first few days. Sometimes he will be too frightened even to use the litter pan, and may cling to the security of your bed and wet the bedclothes. This is normal

GETTING ALONG
Always supervise your pets when they meet for the first time, and before you leave them on their own be certain that they will not harm each other.

behavior and he will soon remember the purpose of the litter pan.

Playing Your kitten will need a lot of love and attention, and since he no longer has siblings to play with, he will turn to you. In effect, you will become his sibling and he will wrestle your hand, kick and gently nibble you. This is normal behavior and the way in which he burns off excess energy. If his bites become firmer, discourage him by saying "No!" firmly or by blowing softly into his face. Don't pull your hand away too quickly as he may clamp down even harder.

Until he is used to you, don't thrust your hand in his face as you might with a puppy. Hands are large objects and may frighten him. Always talk softly—baby talk is very effective—and move slowly. Gentle petting and grooming are called for, and rough-housing with him should be done carefully.

Meeting other pets Don't turn your new kitten loose with your other pets as soon as he arrives home. His most important needs are to feel secure, eat normally, and use his litter pan. When ready, one way

to introduce him to other cats and dogs is to put him in a room with a screen door so he can meet the other pets without being able to fight. Another method is to set up a temporary cage in a room where other pets can sniff noses with him but cannot have any spats.

If you don't wish to try these methods, turn him loose in the house after he has had a few days to settle in. See how the other animals accept him. It is normal for them to hiss and spit at him. A kitten will not fight, and he is used to his own mother hissing at him and even kicking him away when she has decided he no longer needs to nurse. Unless hopelessly trapped, your kitten will simply walk away.

FOREVER AFTER
Once your adult cat has adjusted to his new home, he will provide you with years of pleasure and companionship.

SETTLING IN continued

Adopting an adult cat If your new pet is an adult, transport him home in a carrier, where he will be safe and secure. Don't be tempted to let him loose in the car. He will most likely be fearful and could scratch or bite you while he is trying to hide.

Once home, don't turn him loose in the house. Your primary concern is to ensure that he has a safe refuge away from people and other pets. Unlike a kitten, he will not cry for his siblings, but he will probably seek out a hiding place in his room.

Provide him with water and food dishes and a litter pan in his room. If he hides under a piece of furniture, place a cat bed or small blanket there for his comfort. He will not use a pillow or cat bed in the open until he feels secure.

Cats don't like change. They especially dislike moving to a new house or being confronted with any new furniture in their old one. So your adult cat has a double burden to contend with because he has lost both his old home and his old familiar furnishings.

The new home There is no yardstick by which you can measure how long it will take for your cat to

settle in. Some will come around within a few days and others may take weeks or even months. Patience is the key to helping him adjust.

Avoid talking loudly and don't make sudden movements. Cats dislike noise and raised voices almost as much as they dislike a new house. Don't pick him up against his will and don't force him to come out of hiding. This will frighten him and he may not be able to trust you again.

As long as he is eating food, drinking water and using his litter pan, you have won half the battle. If he is too afraid to come to you, try sitting quietly on the floor and talking softly to him. On floor level, you no longer appear to be a giant and he is more likely to approach you. Drag a piece of ribbon or string slowly in front of his hiding place and he may creep out. Most important, let him come to you. A sudden move to scoop him up will only send him back into hiding.

Until he feels secure enough to move about his room without fleeing when you enter it, you should not give him access to the rest of the house. But as soon as he does feel at home in the room and with you, open the door and let him explore on his own.

Meeting other pets If you have other cats or dogs, it's not a good idea to turn your new cat loose with them. Either keep your cat in a separate room while he learns about his new home, or try setting up a large cage in one of the rooms and placing him in it.

The cage should be set against a wall so that he can retreat to a safe position when his new friends come to make his acquaintance. You can expect some hissing, growling and raised hair on both sides. This is normal so don't worry. This stranger has invaded the property of your other pets so such reactions are completely natural.

After the noises and fluffed tails have subsided, either within a day or two or some weeks, open the door to the cage and let him out, but only

WHERE TO SLEEP?
You can provide your new cat with a bed, but if he decides he would prefer to sleep elsewhere, there is little you can do about it. Just accept it, and make the bed he chooses as comfortable as you can.

with you standing guard. Don't ever leave him unprotected while you are away from home until you are absolutely certain that all your pets are mixing well together.

You might find that your own cat, who was in charge, makes a sudden shift in the pecking order and allows the newcomer or one of your other cats to dominate the group. You might also find that your other pets react to this intrusion by developing

bad habits of their own. They may be more forceful in their play, use the carpet for a litter pan or even mark their territory by spraying. Neutered males and spayed females are both capable of spraying when stressed.

When you adopt an adult cat, you should expect it to take time for him to feel completely secure. Be patient as he will come around eventually. An added bonus is that he will probably already be house-trained.

HOW TO HOLD A CAT

Your cat will enjoy being held as long as he feels secure in your arms. Hold him firmly and confidently and he'll soon become quite relaxed. With strange cats, however, the task is trickier. Never hold him by the tail as this could injure his spinal column.

You can safely pick up a kitten by the scruff of the neck, while at the same time supporting him by placing your hand underneath his body. But never pick up an adult cat this way.

To pick up an older kitten or a small cat, support his weight from underneath with one hand and hold him securely to your chest with the other hand. If he is a very large cat, pick him up by placing one arm under his body from the rear, with your hand coming up between his front legs. Support his weight with the other hand and hold him firmly to prevent him from freeing himself. With a cat that is struggling to escape, you will need to hold him by the scruff of the neck with your other arm under his body to take the weight. Never pick a cat up by his legs or his tail, and don't let children pick him up this way either.

Children and cats A child and an older cat will usually work out a method acceptable to both. The cat may simply let himself go limp and allow the child to carry him around plopped over the child's arms with the rest of his body dangling. Teach children to handle small kittens carefully, always using two hands and supporting the weight from beneath the kitten's bottom.

Giving medicine Most people have difficulty holding a squirming cat while it is being treated or given medication. Place the cat on a smooth bench or work surface. He will be easier to handle and less likely to scratch you if the bench is at about sink height. If you can get your cat to lie down, you may be able to hold him down firmly by the scruff of the neck and the shoulders so that he can't wriggle out of your grasp. Avoid pushing down on his back or his hindquarters as this will make him rake with his hind legs. If he is sitting, hold him firmly by the scruff of the neck with one hand and put your other arm around his body, holding him close to you by the chest. Beware of scratches with this approach.

The towel trick To prevent those sharp claws from doing anyone an injury while you treat any part of your cat's head, take him firmly by the scruff of his neck and wrap a thick towel around him so that only his head is showing. Tuck the edge of the towel in as you would a turban. Don't release your hold on the scruff of your cat's neck until the eye or ear treatment has been completed successfully.

INDOOR VERSUS OUTDOOR

You will need to consider the type of companionship you want from your cat, where you live and your lifestyle before deciding whether yours should be an indoor or an outdoor cat.

If you live close to busy streets, you might consider keeping your cat strictly indoors for his own safety. However, if you have a reasonably large yard or live on a farm, you may prefer to have an indoor/outdoor cat. The choice is yours but there are certain points to consider before making the decision.

OUTSIDE IN

It's never too late to change your cat's lifestyle to being a totally indoor cat. Just keep him inside and, over only a short time, he will easily adapt to his new life in the home and to being confined.

Companionship If your cat is kept strictly indoors, he will quickly become totally domesticated and happy and be a complete companion to you. You can place a carpeted shelf on a windowsill and open the window to give him the benefit of fresh air and sunshine through the safety of a screen. And he can chatter at the birds as they flit by without harming them.

On the other hand, if you allow your cat to be an indoor/outdoor cat, he will never fully develop into a domestic companion. For his own protection, he must retain many of the wild instincts necessary for survival. Although you may prefer this, be aware that he may bring some of these instincts home. Even if he is neutered, he may still mark his territory every time he enters the house. He does this by spraying against a door, a piece of furniture or even your bed. All outdoor females, intact or spayed, may also engage in this behavior and, occasionally, the totally indoor cat may as well.

Outdoor life

If you have an enclosed yard, your cat may enjoy spending time outside, but keep in mind that he is not totally safe as he can easily wander out of the yard and other cats can wander in.

The dangers your cat may encounter outdoors range from being attacked by neighboring cats or dogs to being struck by an automobile. He is vulnerable to blood poisoning from an abscess, the result of a bite from a cat or dog. But bites are not always noticed until infection has spread through his bloodstream, .

Farm life If yours is a working cat on a farm or ranch, he will have to learn the pitfalls of livestock and moving vehicles on his own as there is little you can do to help him.

Make sure he is current on his vaccinations and that he has a dry, comfortable place to sleep.

Check with your vet as to available flea-control products, such as a monthly injection or drops placed on your cat's neck. Alternatively, a flea collar will help. Dust both him and his bedding with flea powder.

Unaltered cats If your cat is unaltered and goes outdoors, you will need to check him frequently for wounds inflicted by other tomcats. If females have kittens, they should be provided with a secure retreat to protect the young from predators—their father might be one.

Nature has her own way of controlling the population and she does this by eliminating kittens and cats through disease or by compelling invading tomcats to reduce the number of kittens by killing them. So, if you have an outdoor cat, you should ensure that he is neutered.

THE OUTDOOR LIFE
There are both pleasures and perils with an outdoor lifestyle. It is impossible to keep your cat free from fleas and worms if he is allowed outdoors. You will be fighting a losing battle trying to rid your house of fleas as well, because he will reinfest himself—and your home—each time he mixes with other cats.

TRAINING YOUR CAT

Although some people do performance-train their cats, it is time-consuming and there's no guarantee of success. On the other hand, behavioral training is essential for your cat's safety and well-being.

Don't try to turn your cat into a dog. If you want a pet to sit, roll over, or come on command, a cat is not for you. You can train him to come for meals (all of the time) and when you call (most of the time)—success will depend entirely on his mood.

Household safety The most important things to train your cat for are

DISTRACTIONS
You can entice your cat to come by dangling a favorite toy or offering him food, but this doesn't mean he will obey every time.

activities that might endanger either him or your belongings. You don't want him making the stovetop his habitat as he may be burned if it happens to be hot. And your guests might take a dim view of sharing your supper when it's been prepared with the help of the cat.

Begin training your cat as soon as he is old enough to try and jump up on the stove. A squirt with a spray bottle is effective, but only if you can stand guard in the kitchen 24 hours a day. For those other times, cover the surface of the stove top with foil or metal pots and pans. Not only will it be difficult for him to find a place to sit, but the noise they make

DETERRENTS
To discourage your cat from scratching the furniture, attach orange peel to it—he will hate the smell and quickly back away.

when he jumps up should send him scampering. Cats hate noise and quickly learn to avoid making any. As a matter of course, you might cover the top of your stove, refrigerator and microwave with pots to discourage him from making them his lairs.

Cat flaps If you would like your cat to come and go at will, a cat flap may be the answer. To train him to use the cat flap, prop it completely open. Leave him in the house and position yourself outside, directly in

using the partially closed flap without hesitation, move on to the final step, which is to repeat the process with the flap down.

Flower pots To prevent your cat from digging up the soil in a flower pot or using it as a litter pan, cover the earth with small stones or "cat pepper". If he persists, consider hanging the plant well out of his reach. Never use mothballs as a deterrent as they could be fatal to him if eaten.

On the furniture It is not practical to allow your cat access to one chair and forbid access to another. He will not understand the difference between the two chairs and you will end up with a nervous and unhappy cat. However, if you don't want him to

scratch your furniture, cover his favorite scratching areas with clear heavy plastic, available at pet stores, or tape orange peel to areas he likes to scratch. Another suggestion is to place a small scratching post at either end of the couch or chair.

OFF LIMITS
If you are unable to keep your cat from your stove, cover the top with syrup or another sticky substance. Cats, such as this Siamese, hate anything sticky on them and it won't take long for her to decide the area is off limits.

LITTER-PAN TRAINING
A kitten will usually take to using a litter pan naturally. If he uses a rug or bedding as a litter pan, deter him from repeating the offense by lightly spraying the area with cologne. Most cats like to lick perfume and won't soil where they lick.

front of the flap. Then call to him with his favorite food at hand. Once he is through, go inside and repeat the process until he willingly goes through the cat flap. Then, lower the flap halfway so he is forced to push it aside in order to pass through. Again, call him and offer a treat when he goes through. Once he is

BEING A RESPONSIBLE OWNER

Before acquiring or selling a cat, there are a number of practical and legal issues you should consider. Possibly the most important is to ensure that he is both registered and fitted with clear identification.

If you have a pedigreed cat, you should have been given his papers when you acquired him. These consist of a registration certificate or application for registration completed by the breeder as well as a pedigree showing his family tree.

If you have a mixed-breed cat, it's still a good idea to register him. Almost all of the cat-registering associations offer registration in the household pet category. Their only condition is that any cat so registered not be used for breeding—a requirement aimed at reducing the number of unwanted kittens. As well as the major associations, there are a number of independent groups that register mixed breeds. These can be located through advertisements in cat magazines.

In some states in the US, cats are considered feral and, as such, have no rights under the relevant state's laws. Although rarely enforced, you should make inquiries to be certain of your cat's status.

Advantages The advantages of having a registration certificate on your cat are many. First, it identifies him as to sex, color, eye color, hair length, and age. In the case of the purebred, it registers his breed as

IDENTIFICATION

If your cat ventures outdoors, there is a huge variety of tags available to attach to his collar for identification purposes. The break-away collar is recommended for safety. However, if the collar does break away, he will lose his identifications. Another alternative is to have your vet implant a microchip that will identify him to any vet or animal shelter with the appropriate scanning device.

well. If he goes outdoors and is picked up by another person, it will help identify him as your cat. If you have multiple cats and meet with an accident, it will serve to identify your cats and make it easier to place them in care until you return home.

In an extreme case, if your cat wreaks havoc in a neighbor's garden, and that neighbor then harms him, the certificate will serve as proof of ownership in the event that you take the neighbor to court for damages.

Breeder or pet store If you buy a cat from a breeder or a pet store, you should ask about a health guarantee. The ethical person will give you a certain number of days during which time you should have the cat examined by your own vet. If he is not completely healthy, you can return him to the seller and receive a full refund.

The pound If you acquire a cat from the pound, or from a rescue center, you will be bound by their rules, and most will stipulate that any animal leaving their kennel

FOR SALE
You should always take your new kitten or cat to a vet for a checkup, regardless of where you acquired him. He should be in good health and free from any parasites. Even if it just seems like a cold, don't dismiss it. Take him to the vet because neglect can result in lifelong snuffles from rhinitis.

must be neutered or spayed, regardless of age. In the US, they are now neutering and spaying kittens at eight weeks of age. However, in Britain, they advise against neutering or spaying until cats are six months old.

Spaying or neutering Unless you are planning to use your cat for breeding purposes, it is important to have him or her desexed (see p. 116). There are already far too many unwanted kittens looking for homes. Your vet will advise you on

BEING A RESPONSIBLE OWNER continued

the best age to have it done. Generally though, while a female can be spayed when she is only a few months old, you should wait until a male is six months old.

The cost of desexing your cat varies from place to place, but it pales in comparison with the potential cost of treating him for wounds as a result of fighting other tomcats, or replacing your carpet or furniture because of spraying.

If you are on a limited income and cannot afford the full price, ask your town authorities and local vets about a low-cost neutering program. If you cannot find one in your area, start one up with a few friends.

Phone the local vets, choose a name for your group, print up letterhead and find a vet willing to perform low-cost neutering.

CHOOSING A PEDIGREE

When purchasing pedigreed cats, details of a minimum of three generations should be supplied. If you plan to show, a minimum of five generations is now considered mandatory.

A full day's bookings will give the vet a worthwhile return for his efforts.

Selling your kitten Before a kitten is sold, he should have received at least his first vaccination and instructions should be given as to when his second is due. If selling him at a pet price—not for breeding or showing—you don't need to supply papers. Often, though, papers will be given upon proof from a vet that the cat has been neutered or spayed. At other times, breeders will issue the papers and check the space to indicate the kitten is still to be neutered or spayed.

If you are selling him as a show cat or for breeding purposes, then he will command a higher price and you are bound to provide his papers as well. There is no reason why you shouldn't have all documents ready to go, so a buyer should never accept a cat unless all the relevant papers are ready to be handed over at the time of sale.

Unforeseen events Make provisions for your cat in case of your unexpected hospitalization or death. Any animals confined in the house may starve to death, so be sure to leave written word with a friend, relative or neighbor so they can gain entry and take care of your pets should the need arise.

Choosing a vet When choosing a vet, it is not only important to find one who likes cats but also to find one who will work with you in keeping your pet healthy. It is important to locate a vet who will persist with examinations and tests in order to establish your pet's problem. After all, you live with your cat and know his normal behavior better than

BE PREPARED
Make sure somebody will remember to look after your cat, if you ever have an accident.

anyone else. Unless your cat is sick, you'll need to take him to the vet only once each year for his checkup and annual boosters and vaccinations.

Quarantine If you are moving to another country, your cat may need to be quarantined. Check with the relevant authorities about the quarantine laws in that country..

CARING
FOR
CATS

When you take a cat into your life, you must be prepared to provide for her every need, just as you would with a baby. Having the right equipment will make life easier for you both, but don't rush out and empty the shelves of the local pet store. Start with just the basics and add things as you find you need them to keep your new companion safe and healthy. Cats are very self-sufficient, so don't be daunted. The main thing is to provide her with a safe environment. Think of her as a toddler and take the same precautions you would with a child, such as locking cabinets with dangerous contents and blocking off danger zones that, inevitably, seem to have a fatal attraction.

HOUSING A CAT

It is important to provide a safe and comfortable home for your cat. You should take precautions to reduce the number of accidents that could occur in your home, and you must be sure she has her own haven in which to rest.

ring pillow

A cozy place to sleep You can make a comfortable sleeping place for your cat by placing a ring pillow—a round, stuffed pillow, with sides about 4 inches (10 cm) high—on a piece of furniture, preferably against a wall. She wants the security of being above floor level and with a solid wall at her back. If she has a short or a fine coat and needs extra warmth in winter, a lamp nearby with a low-wattage bulb will supply warmth. Make sure it is securely fastened so that it can't tip over.

If you don't mind having her in the kitchen, a pillow on top of the refrigerator or the washer or dryer makes a good comfort station. Again, she is up high, and the heat from these appliances will keep her warm.

She may decide that your bed or an upholstered chair is her cup of tea, so provide her with a pillow or small blanket for those areas.

HER OWN PRIVATE IGLOO
Cats do a lot of sleeping so they need a safe place to relax fully with no worries of children or other household pets.

A pillow or other bedding on the floor of the closet may suit her very well. Leave the door slightly ajar. She won't feel threatened because it is dark and quiet. Or give her a shelf in a closet. Again, you should place comfortable bedding there.

Keeping her safe It's impossible to ensure that your house is totally safe for your cat, but start by keeping all medicines in a locked cabinet. Household cleaning agents should also be safely behind locked doors. When running a bath, keep the door closed so that she won't fall in. If fully grown, she will hurt only her dignity. If she is a kitten, she may drown. For the same reason, always keep the toilet lid closed.

Be especially careful when opening the oven door as the aromas of food baking may attract her to jump in. While cooking on the stove, either keep her out of the kitchen or watch her closely. Not only can she suffer burns on her feet from a burner still radiating heat, but she may singe her tail or whiskers on a lit burner. Always use a securely fastened fire screen in front of an open fire.

Always check that the washer and dryer are cat-free before turning them on. Before opening windows, make sure that the screens are securely fastened. Remember, cats don't always land on their feet.

wicker basket

cat sock

bean bag

EQUIPMENT FOR CATS

Before you bring your new cat home, make sure you have purchased the essentials: food bowls, litter tray, carrying cage and bedding. There is a huge choice of products on the market, so choose wisely, then add to your equipment as the need arises.

diatomite *recycled paper litter* *litter made from rice husks* *shredded newspaper*

Litter The type of litter you choose for your cat depends entirely on how much you want to spend and how fussy you are about sand, clay, wood shavings and such being tracked through your house.

An economical material for litter is newspaper. Simply line the pan with a section from the newspaper and then cover with strips torn from another section. After the cat uses the litter pan, it is easy to roll up the entire newspaper and dispose of it. This avoids unsightly litter being tracked throughout your house, and it also minimizes odor as the urine is removed from the house, along with her bowel movements.

When using a scoop to remove solids from normal litter or clay, too often the urine-soaked litter remains for days at a time. This not only results in an offensive odor that will soon permeate your house but your cat very often will not want to use the litter pan. Cats do not like to be dirty or have wet feet. If the pan has

litter tray

poop scoop

wet litter in it, she may well decide that your bedspread or a corner of the carpet make fine—and dry—litter pans.

After you have disposed of the contents of the pan (the frequency will depend on the number of cats using it and the odor), make sure that you thoroughly clean the inside and outside of it, using a non-toxic cleaner. If you use a strong cleaning agent, make sure that you rinse the pan completely so that no residual effects of the cleaner can harm her.

Litter tray The size of your cat's litter tray depends on how large she is and if she will be sharing it with any other cats. You can choose a plastic litter tray from several sizes at any grocery or pet store.

It's also a good idea to keep a few disposable cardboard trays on hand. These are useful for short trips with your cat. Or if you have a friend coming by to take care of her while you are away from home, it makes it easier for your friend if the litter tray can be thrown out, contents and all.

Litter trays also come with hoods or are completely enclosed with just a small opening for your cat to enter. Privacy is especially important when there are both dogs and cats in the household. The problem with this type of litter tray is that your cat will very often splash urine against the sides of the enclosure, which will make even more work for you in cleaning not only the tray, but also the enclosure.

EQUIPMENT FOR CATS continued

metal water dish

plastic water dish

ceramic dish

plastic-double feeder

Bowls and saucers Your cat will need bowls for both water and dry food, and a flat saucer for moist or wet food. If there are other cats in the house, or if you are feeding outdoor cats, a water feeder and a dispenser for dry food are excellent. These can hold a larger amount of water and food than bowls, and have protective covers to keep the contents fresher and free from dirt and dust. A water feeder is also useful if you are away from home for several hours at a time, because it means your cat will not go thirsty if she knocks over her water source.

scratching post

Scratching posts and pads A scratching post or pad (a post that rests on the floor) is one of the essential items you need to purchase if your cat is to remain indoors. An indoor/outdoor cat, on the other hand, will simply use the trunk of a tree. Because she likes a good full stretch when scratching, the post should be taller than she is when stretching her body to full length and raising her front legs.

A post covered with tightly woven carpet is preferable to a loosely woven one, and a good choice is indoor/outdoor carpet. Another favorite is a sturdy log or orange crate. Or you can purchase or make a post or pad with sisal rope. Simply wrap the sisal tightly around a length of wood. This can be either free-standing or nailed to a door frame.

Collars, leashes and harnesses
If your cat is always indoors, she will not need a collar. If you want her to wear one for decorative purposes, or in case she slips outside and is found, or if she is an indoor/outdoor cat, then make sure the collar has the break-away feature to keep her from being strangled if it becomes snagged on the branch of a tree.

A leash is needed only if you want to train your cat to take walks with you. The leash should be of a light material and, given that your adult cat may range from 5 to 25 lb (2 to 11 kg), it should be suitable for her size and weight. It should never be fastened to any collar.

Only a figure-8 harness, made expressly for cats, should be used with the leash. A dog harness is not suitable and she might run away if she can easily slip out of her collar.

SAFE HARNESS
The figure-8-type harness is made specially for cats and will restrain your cat with no risk of choking her.

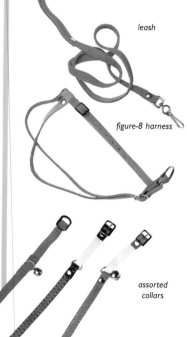

leash

figure-8 harness

assorted
collars

Grooming equipment Your cat will need her own combs and brushes. The types you buy will depend on whether she has a short or long coat and fine or thick hair. Cotton swabs for ear-cleaning are also a must, as well as scissors or clippers made especially for trimming claws.

Cat flaps If she is allowed outside, a cat flap makes an excellent door for your cat. These range from models that can be fitted to a screen door, to solid wooden ones.

Some cat flaps can be opened only by an electronic chip on her collar that operates the door as she approaches. This is a good choice if she is the type of cat that invites other cats home for lunch. It also serves to stop any potential predators, such as small dogs or wildlife, from entering.

Beds and baskets Since cats spend so much time sleeping, it's important to provide them with a bed. It should be big enough for her to stretch out in when she is fully grown, and enclosed on at least three sides for coziness and a sense of security.

Baskets and beds come in wicker, plastic or fiberglass. Or you can make one yourself by lining a cardboard box with sides high enough to exclude drafts. A soft blanket or pillow placed inside will ensure her comfort.

One popular bed is a bean bag that is filled with polystyrene and covered with a removable washable material. Another favorite is a ring, or donut, pillow.

Toys There are many cat toys on the market. Although the best ones have you attached, your cat will need toys for when you're away or too busy to play with her.

A large paper bag on its side on the floor is the source of endless games. When purchasing cat toys, make sure that any you purchase are free of small attachments. These can come off easily and be accidentally swallowed. A good rule of thumb is to ask yourself if the toy is safe for a human baby. If not, then it is probably not safe for your cat.

Cages A cage to confine your cat is a good idea if you have guests who are not fond of cats on their laps or if your cat is ill and needs to be kept in the one place. The cage should be large enough to accommodate her litter tray. Use a kennel or adapt your child's playpen or crib by placing a lid on it. In the case of the crib, cover the sides with hardware cloth, or wire.

Carrying cases A carrying case is an essential piece of equipment.

They can range from inexpensive cardboard types to designer cases. Your cat should be confined to a case when traveling by car, train or airplane, and should always be taken to the vet in one. A cat is not safe in the vet's examining room on your lap or on a leash. Even if the other animals present in the waiting room cannot actually reach her to harm her, she may think they can, and this can cause her needless anxiety and stress when she may already be feeling ill.

FEEDING YOUR CAT

Although all commercial cat foods are nutritionally suitable, your cat will appreciate it if fresh food is included in her diet. It will also make life easier if her food is served in the right place and in the right dish.

PRIVATE DINING
Set aside a special place to feed your cat where she can relax and feel safe while she eats. Cats take a while to consume their meal, rather than gulping it down as dogs do.

What, when and how What to feed your cat, how often and in what type of container will depend entirely on the type of cat she is, her age, and whether she eats indoors or outdoors.

Feeding your kitten Usually a mother cat will wean her kittens onto pre-chewed morsels of field mice and birds when they are about five weeks of age.

If you are raising a litter of kittens totally indoors, start weaning them at five weeks by giving them a mixture of cereal, egg yolk and either goat's milk or lactose-free evaporated milk every four hours. Very often though, they may have already started eating the food you give their mother. Don't worry as this will not hurt them.

Never give cow's milk to kittens or in fact to any cat. Cats do not have the enzyme necessary to digest the milk sugar lactose properly and could develop diarrhea.

Variety Accustom your cat to different flavors of wet and dry food. You can't go wrong with any of the flavors of packaged dry food or canned moist food. Experiment until you know her favorite foods, but don't be surprised if she later turns her nose up at them. With such a variety available, it's simply a matter of trying another flavor.

Cats like a change in diet and you are bound to give them table treats although you should do so only occasionally. They can digest almost all of our foods, except milk, cheese and chocolate. Do not feed her a diet of red fish either, unless it has been specially prepared by a pet food manufacturer, as it can be harmful.

A change in her diet may bring on diarrhea or vomiting for up to one week, but these symptoms don't necessarily mean that the new food doesn't agree with her. Such problems should always be checked out with your vet, even when they coincide with a change in your cat's diet. The best plan is to make changes to her diet gradually, over a seven-day period. Cut up some kidney, heart or liver, or give her uncooked chicken necks to supplement commercial foods.

Necessary nutrients
Government regulations in most countries require that any cat food purchased from a grocery or pet store be completely nutritious and meet the specific needs of cats. Specially developed scientific formulas are available in many areas, generally however, through vets or selective pet stores.

Your cat will require those formulated foods only if she has a special health

scientific formula

meat-flavored biscuits

fish-flavored biscuits

FEEDING YOUR CAT continued

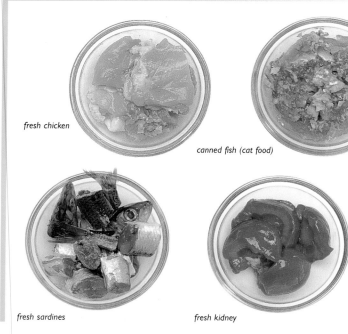

fresh chicken

canned fish (cat food)

fresh sardines

fresh kidney

problem, and your vet will instruct you as to the type of food your cat requires and where to purchase it.

The dining room Your cat's eating area should be located where she has some privacy, but do not place her food and water dishes near her litter pan. If you have a dog living in the house, find an elevated location for your cat's food. No self-respecting dog can resist the aroma of cat food.

Food dishes It's best to give your cat wet food on a flat saucer. Cats hate the sensation of their whiskers touching the sides of a bowl, so will very often not finish their food. Dry food can be fed in a bowl, however; if you watch closely, you'll see she takes a piece of food from the bowl, and places it on a flat surface before eating it. If she lives solely on dry food, then it is best to provide it in a self-feeding dispenser.

If you have more than one cat, they might eat from the same dish. If you have a water dish in the house for a dog, your cat can use it too. Keep water containers filled and fresh. A self-watering canister will help keep water free from dust, but clean the container regularly.

Quantities Feed cats twice a day with an amount that depends on their size and liveliness. To ascertain whether she is the proper weight, run your hands down her backbone and across her hip bones. You should not be able to feel her bones clearly through the flesh. Alternatively, weigh her once a month for three or four months and consult your vet as to whether she falls within normal parameters.

Not hungry If your cat doesn't want to eat, or if she is sick, tempt her by warming her food to blood heat. This increases its palatability by about 40 percent. Or try spreading some food on her paws. In severe cases, make a liquid solution of the food and squirt it into her mouth with an eye dropper.

DO IT HER WAY
Your cat may want to take her time over the meal, perhaps going away and returning several times, so don't whisk the food away as soon as she leaves. In hot weather, you must pick up and throw away the food before it spoils, but in mild weather, most foods can be left out through the day or night.

CLEANING YOUR CAT

While cats are very clean animals, a little help from you with her mouth and other hard-to-reach places will keep her in tip-top condition. If you start cleaning your cat when she is young she may even come to enjoy your attentions.

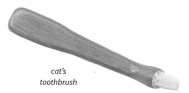

cat's toothbrush

GOOD FRIENDS
While mothers lick their kittens to clean them, when older cats indulge in mutual grooming, it may be more a case of being sociable.

A cat is one of the cleanest creatures on earth, and spends a large part of her waking hours washing herself. She can go through life very nicely without ever having a bath, as daily combing and brushing will suffice. But if you are a cat fancier and plan on showing her, you must always present her in tip-top shape, and groom and wash her regularly.

She will also need a bath if she has a foreign or toxic substance on her coat that must be washed off immediately. Or you may need to remove soot if she has been playing in the fireplace. Or if she is an indoor/outdoor cat, she may have an accumulation of household dust or dirt that needs to be washed off.

Your cat's saliva could either turn your cat's dark coat a reddish color, or her white or light-colored coat a yellowish color. Sunlight may also affect the color of her coat. So no matter how many times you wash her, you may never be able to keep her coat completely stain-free.

Cleaning her ears Either before or after her bath, clean her ears with a cotton swab dipped in plain warm water or an ear-cleaning solution available from your vet. Just remove dirt and excess wax from inside the ear flap. Never probe the ear canal.

Cleaning her face The rest of her face can be cleaned with a soft cloth dipped into warm water. You might even make this part of her daily routine to freshen her face and also to remove any matter that collects in the corners of her eyes.

To remove tear-track stains, paint them with either cornstarch or boric acid mixed to a paste with a little peroxide. Be especially careful when working anywhere near her eyes. Apply the paste with a cotton swab or cotton ball. Rinse and dry. The lightest smear of petroleum jelly will make the area more stain-resistant.

Although tear tracks should be washed off regularly with water, you will only need to use the paste every few times. If not washed daily, she could develop deep furrows that can actually fester simply from the tears running down her face.

Dental and gum care Your vet should check your cat's mouth on her yearly physical and will usually clean your cat's teeth. In the meantime, you should regularly check her teeth and gums for soreness, tartar or diseased or broken teeth.

You can help ward off tooth decay and gum infection by cleaning your cat's teeth on a regular basis. It's

GUM MASSAGE
Prevention is better than cure. So take the time regularly to massage your cat's gums and teeth to help prevent disease and the buildup of tartar.

easiest to do this if you start the practice when she's a kitten as she will quickly become accustomed to it. Begin by wrapping a small bit of gauze around your finger and then gently rubbing on and around the teeth and along the gums. Then graduate to an actual cat toothbrush (make sure you use one made expressly for cats) and cat tooth-paste. Loss of appetite, drooling, or reluctance to eat sometimes indicates that there is a dental problem.

BATHING AND DRYING

If you anticipate that your cat will need regular bathing, perhaps because she is a longhaired white with a show career ahead of her, start giving her wet baths while she's still a kitten and is small enough to be held easily.

Wet baths It is best to try to give your cat a bath by yourself. Another pair of hands can panic her and increase her struggle to free herself. The ideal spot for her bath is any sizable sink or bowl that is about waist-high to you. The height most comfortable is that of the kitchen sink. Cats are easily frightened if you place them in a low-lying basin and loom over them. You will also find it more difficult to hold and control them in this awkward position.

Have all of your shampoos, rinses or flea-dip preparations ready, as well as a soft towel for washing her face and a large towel for the initial drying of her coat. Make sure they are placed within easy reach of you but out of reach of your cat. Initially, she will attempt to attach herself to anything in close range in order to escape the water.

The choice of shampoos is up to you and depends upon her coat type. A shampoo containing a whitener is recommended for white cats, or if she has a skin or flea problem, you should use a chemical flea shampoo. You may also use a mild human shampoo, such as one you would use for babies, and finish off with a good-quality conditioner.

If your cat has grease on her coat, use a bay rum spirit conditioner or mineral spirits to remove it. If she has stains and has a pale coat, then a surgical spirit is essential.

Don't worry about washing inside her ears as this is best done separately. Some experts advise putting a cotton ball inside her ears so that water will not penetrate. This is not a good idea as it could alarm her. Others say to put petroleum jelly around her eyes so that shampoo will not enter. This, too, is bad advice as it will not fully prevent the suds from getting into her eyes. The jelly will bother her to the extent that she will keep trying to wipe it off and so interfere with your being able to bathe her. She may also spread it through her coat.

Place a rubber mat or towel in the bottom of the sink. Fill it with lukewarm water that comes up to her shoulders. Place her in the water facing away from you. Never let her face toward you as she can stretch her legs out much farther than you expect and claw into your clothing or arms.

If you place all four of her feet into the water at once, she will generally settle down. Then put one hand across her shoulders, very gently (she will struggle mightily if the pressure is too great), and use the other hand to wet her down and apply the shampoo. Avoid grasping the back of her neck. Although this will calm down a kitten as she is accustomed to her mother subduing her in that fashion, the adult cat will only struggle more.

Move slowly and talk softly. It is not necessary to apply shampoo directly onto her face as you can more safely and easily wash her ears and face at another time with the cloth dipped into the bath water and wrung out nearly dry.

After you have lathered her, rinse the shampoo off with either glassfuls of water or a rubber spray hose. Be sure to rinse all of the shampoo out of her coat as even a small amount left will cause her to froth at the mouth when she starts licking herself after the bath. If a conditioner is used, make sure to thoroughly rinse it off in the same manner. Then gather her up in the towel, wrap it around her securely, and carry her to a draft-free room.

She may tremble with fear or anxiety, so sit down with her and let the towel absorb the excess moisture while you speak reassuringly to her.

Dry baths If you don't feel up to giving her a wet bath, if she has an infection, or if the weather is cold, then it's probably best to give your cat a dry bath. There are a number of dry shampoo products on the market. Sprinkle the powder through her coat and brush it off thoroughly. Use a towel to remove any excess powder. Cats hate anything foreign on their coat, and the powder may irritate her.

dry shampoo

brush

*grooming glove for
longhaired cats*

*plastic flea
combs*

Drying shorthaired cats If it is
a warm day, you can let your shorthaired cat dry naturally in a room.
However, you should make sure all
windows remain closed until she is
completely dry. Any draft, even a
warm one, can be harmful to her.
If it is a cool day you can turn on

brush for detangling
matted hair

blunt-tipped scissors

an electric heater to speed up the process. You could attempt to dry her with a hair dryer if she is a shorthaired companion cat. However, if she is a show cat whose standard calls for a sleek coat lying flat, then the dryer would add too much fullness for her to have much success with judges.

Drying longhaired or medium-haired cats If yours is a long-haired or medium-haired cat, you will have extra work to do as self-drying is not really suitable for her. As she dries, you must continually comb through her coat so that it does not tangle. If you start this process when she is young, you can quickly accustom her to the hair dryer, which will dramatically speed up the process.

Whether drying your cat's coat naturally or with the assistance of a hair dryer, you should continue to comb her coat until it is completely dry. If she won't hold still enough for you to comb her with one hand and hold the dryer with the other hand, you will need some assistance. Construct a makeshift holder for the hair dryer, perhaps with a clamp, or purchase an inexpensive dryer and stand from the pet store.

GROOMING

All cat owners will need to spend at least some time grooming their cat. However the length of time you choose to spend will depend on whether she is an indoor or outdoor cat, whether she is longhaired or shorthaired, and whether you plan to show her or just have her as a companion.

Grooming shorthaired cats

Accustom your shorthaired cat to combing every three or four days as soon as you acquire her. Use a comb with small, close teeth. Start combing at the back of her neck and work your way down to her tail, following the fall of her hair. Be especially careful around her hindquarters and other such sensitive areas. Then repeat the combing using a hard rubber brush.

The natural oils as found on the palms of your hands are great for making her coat lie flat. Daily petting

GROOMING SHORTHAIRS

After an initial combing with a fine-toothed metal comb, go over the coat once again with a hard rubber brush. Always work in the direction the hair falls naturally.

by you can be just about as effective as brushing her. If you wish, finish off her shorthaired coat by running a damp chamois or a silk scarf over it.

Grooming longhaired cats

If you have a longhaired cat, then you have your work cut out, and if you plan to show her, you will need to put in extra effort. Aside from the length of time required to comb her as she dries after a bath, you can expect to be her personal scrub nurse every day.

She may not be able to avoid clumps of fecal matter on her coat no matter how hard she tries. The very fact that she has long hair around her rear end and britches (the back of her legs) makes it

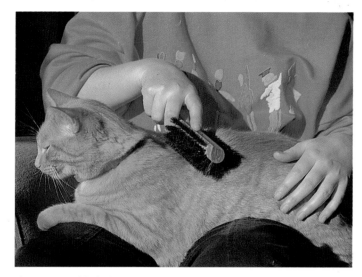

almost impossible for her to avoid becoming messy.

You will need to regularly inspect your cat's rear end to see if she is clean. If not, stand her on a bench

with her rear end hanging over a basin, and wash the stained area with warm water and a mild soap, being sure to rinse it thoroughly. If she has just a small amount clinging

GROOMING continued

to her britches, you can pluck it off and then powder her—with cornstarch if she is a light-colored cat or Fuller's earth if she is dark-colored cat—as you comb through the hair.

If she is one of the tailless breeds —such as the Manx, Cymric or Japanese Bobtail—she may have the same problem, even if she is short-haired. Without a full tail, she lacks the "nipping" ability to sever the feces neatly and cleanly and instead, it will often stick to her legs. Since she has no tail, you can easily see if she needs attention and clean her up as prescribed for the longhaired cat.

To make it easier to groom her long hair, sprinkle either cornstarch or Fuller's earth through her coat. The powder will loosen the tangles and make it easier for the teeth of the comb to slip through. Use a wide-toothed comb for removing tangles. Pay special attention to her britches, tail and stomach. You can reach her stomach by turning her upside down on your lap. Make this an enjoyable time and combine affection with play (such as dangling your necklace or chain for her).

Even with daily combing, her coat may be of such a consistency that she will get a greasy buildup on her tummy area and mats will form. To remove these, use blunt-tipped scissors. Separate the mat as much as you can with your fingers. Then, place one of your fingers against her skin so that you will not stab her as you cut off the mat.

If for some reason you have not kept up with her daily grooming and she develops severe mats that you are unable to remove, you must seek professional help from a cat groomer or your vet right away. If not taken care of, the mats will twist into such a snarl that they will pinch her skin quite painfully.

You'll need to use a soft brush for her ruff (the hair framing her neck) as this should stand out away from her body. And pay special attention to her toes.

Longhaired cats grow toe tufts that are beautiful to see but can tangle just as her body hair does. Finish off her longhaired coat by brushing or combing her hair the wrong way so that it stands out from her body.

BE REALISTIC

The glamorous longhairs may be irresistibly gorgeous, but be honest with yourself about whether or not you really have the time and the inclination to give such a coat the care it needs to stay in peak condition.

TRIMMING CLAWS AND DECLAWING

While it may be necessary to trim your cat's claws from time to time, declawing is frowned upon and not practiced in most countries in the world. Although it is becoming more and more popular in the US, it should be considered only as a last resort.

SCISSOR OR GUILLOTINE
When trimming claws, you can use either scissor-action or guillotine-action clippers.

Declawing If you are consistent with training methods, and offer your cat a choice of objects on which to claw, there's a good chance that you may prevent her from clawing your furniture. Despite your best efforts, however, she may still persist with her shredding.

Only when all training measures have failed, and the choice is between giving your cat up or having her declawed, should you consider the surgery. Before you do so, ask yourself these questions. Am I planning to keep her forever?

Do I fully understand that she may never be let outdoors again?

A declawed cat has a hard time climbing a tree to escape a dog and cannot defend herself properly if cornered. There are also behavioral changes that may include her refusal to use her litter pan, frequent biting or increased nervousness, loss of balance or less climbing ability and she may take to hiding or be easily startled. She may also take to using her teeth with increasing regularity since she no longer has claws. This makes giving pills, grooming and

bathing extremely hazardous as a wound inflicted by her teeth is more severe than one inflicted by her claws.

If your only recourse is to have her declawed, you should be aware that this is an orthopedic procedure that calls for the removal of the claw and the first bone of each toe. This is similar to an amputation of your fingertips at the first knuckle, and it will be extremely painful for your cat to stand on her mutilated feet until the toes have fully healed.

If the vet performing the surgery is inexperienced, or if the surgery does not go well, recovery can be even more painful for your cat and leave her with residual paw tenderness or lameness for life.

TRIMMING CLAWS

If you plan to keep your cat totally indoors, you may want to keep her claws trimmed to minimize damage to furniture. If you start trimming your cat's claws when she is a kitten, she will discover that it doesn't hurt one bit and will resign herself to the process. It's probably best to trim her claws before you bathe her.

By squeezing her toe between your forefinger and thumb, her claw will be easily extended and can be trimmed with clippers made specially for cats. Be sure to avoid the sensitive pink quick and to remove only the very tip of the claw. Hold her gently and talk softly while clipping. Don't panic and don't raise your voice. A loud, angry or high-pitched voice will only make her more anxious and fearful.

Do not tighten your hold. Pause for a moment, continue to talk quietly and you might even try blowing softly into her face, at the same time saying "no" in a low but firm voice. Tickling behind the ears will often trigger a more amenable mood. Do not let her free until you have trimmed all of her claws, otherwise she will learn that it pays to struggle. She will need her claws clipped only about once a month.

EXTEND CLAWS
Firmly but gently place the cat in your lap, and then press down on the pad to extend the claw.

CLIP CAREFULLY
View the claws from the side and be sure not to cut within $1/10$ inch (2 mm) of the quick.

quick

trimming line

EXERCISE AND PLAY

While cats, especially kittens, don't need to be exercised as dogs do, all cats will enjoy the companionship they sense when you play with them. And it will also strengthen the bond between you.

THE GAME HUNTER
Your kitten's lively imagination can turn almost anything, leaves, balls of paper, feathers or pieces of string, into potential prey as she practices her hunting skills.

POUNCING
Your cat will get all the exercise she needs through her normal everyday activities, but she will love to have you play with her. Set aside some time each day for the pure delight of play.

Your new kitten will eat, sleep and, on waking, run about the house like one possessed. She will make her tail bushy and even leap up on the walls, and this behavior will continue from when she is about six weeks old until she settles down as an adult, although she may still act like a kitten well into adulthood.

While she is still a kitten, she will want to play every waking moment. Don't overtire her though, as you can cause her to feel stressed and possibly retard her growth slightly.

Your kitten will attack her siblings with tooth and claw and you'll wonder how any of them manage to survive kittenhood. Her mother will tolerate the tail-biting and ear-chewing, but will let the kitten know when enough is enough by seizing the baby's neck between her teeth and settling her down.

When you acquire a single kitten, she will want to use you as one of her siblings. Gentle rough-housing is fine, but don't overdo it. Treat her as you would a baby or toddler, but don't swing her up in the air as you might a baby—keep her at lap level or below.

Playtime The best toy is one with you at the other end. Your cat loves to pounce on your toes or fingers as they move underneath the bedcovers. A bit of string, a belt or anything that dangles is appealing to her. A ribbon trailed enticingly across the floor or in front of her hiding place is sure to elicit a delighted pounce and scamper after the trailing end. Or you can make your own fishing pole out of a stick, some fishing line and a bit of cloth attached to the end of the line. You

DOING WHAT COMES NATURALLY
The best scratching post of all is a tree in your garden, but that's only the start of the possibilities a tree presents.

EXERCISE AND PLAY continued

can even make a ball out of aluminum foil, which is light and rolls well. A pipe cleaner shaped in a circle and tossed will result in endless fun for her as she picks it up in her mouth and returns it (or drops it just out of reach, which she thinks is hilarious).

Or take a cardboard box, seal it, and cut holes on the top and sides large enough for her to pass through. Toss a toy or two inside and she will be amused for hours.

Venturing outdoors Your indoor cat can always find plenty of exercise in her home, but if you want to take your indoor cat outside for some sunshine and to smell the roses, you could try to train her to walk on a

THE GREAT OUTDOORS
An outdoor cat, such as this Tonkinese, will have all the exercise she needs chasing leaves and birds, killing rodents and patrolling and marking her territory.

figure-8 leash. Don't consider this proper exercise, though, as she will generally curl herself into a clump so that you have to move her along by gently tugging on the leash.

Outdoor cats If your cat goes outdoors, she will run rapidly after real or imagined prey. To an indoor/outdoor cat, a leaf wafting across the lawn is as attractive as a bird or mouse. As for the working cat, she will develop and retain her muscles and condition by keeping the ranch or farm free of rodents and other vermin.

The indoor/outdoor cat, as well as the completely outdoor cat, gets plenty of exercise as she is compelled to make the rounds of her territory every day. She will leave her mark either by spraying, rubbing her cheek against a tree or building, or leaving scars in tree trunks from her claws. This daily patrol not only keeps her active and busy, but it also keeps her fit.

Aging cats As your cat grows older, she will sleep more and more. In addition to watching her diet, you need to encourage her to play by leaving toys out and setting aside time each and every day to spend with her.

SLOWING DOWN

This elderly cat would be quite happy lazing in a warm spot and moving only to eat and relieve herself. But her health will be better if you encourage her to play and remain active for as long as possible. Some veterans even have short periods of being quite kittenish again.

CAT TRAVEL

There may come a time when your cat simply must undertake a journey. She won't like it, but there are a few things you can do to make the experience less stressful for both of you.

HAVE CAT, WILL TRAVEL

If you must take your cat on a long trip, get her used to her carrying cage by placing her in it for some time each day for a week or so before the journey. Feeding her near it will also help.

Road travel If you have to transport your cat, perhaps because you are moving, always confine her in a suitable carrying cage. If it makes you feel better, when you stop for a rest break offer her food, water and access to a litter pan. Don't be surprised if she refuses all three. Most cats prefer to wait until they reach the motel—or the new home—before eating, drinking or going to the bathroom. Don't worry—she can survive very well during the day.

Rail and air travel If you are shipping cats by rail or air, first check with the carriers and find out their rules for health certificates and suitable shipping containers. It is not advisable to give cats tranquilizers. Some cats can become very aggressive on this type of medication while others become sick. If heavily tranquilized, their vomiting can cause them to drown in their own fluids.

Line the bottom of the shipping container with a good thickness of newspaper and tear up strips of newspaper, filling the container about halfway to the top. This makes an excellent insulator for heat and cold and your cat can burrow into it for security. Should she have to go to the bathroom, she can cover her waste with the strips of paper.

Always make a definite reservation for her with the airline or train carrier and have a back-up plan in

open wire-top carrier

CONTAINERS

When you book your cat in to travel by rail or air, ask if any particular type of container is required. Naturally, it must be strong and able to be locked securely, and the labelling should be clear.

typical airline carrier

mind. Always try for a direct flight with no change of plane or train. Most airlines will not carry pets if the ground temperature at either departure or destination is below 45°F (7°C) or above 80°F (27°C), but you will need to check on this with the airline when you book.

LEAVING YOUR CAT BEHIND

Cats don't like change and don't travel well, so whenever possible make arrangements for your cat to stay at home in her own surroundings and avoid sending her anywhere to board.

TWO'S COMPANY
Young kittens need company. If there are two, at least they will entertain each other, but you still need a pet-sitter to call in once or twice daily to check on their well-being.

Cats don't travel well and much prefer the familiar comforts of their home and surroundings. They will generally be much happier and safer if left at home, but you will also need to consider how long you will be gone, where you live and the state of your finances.

Home alone If your cats live totally outdoors, then oversize self-feeders for both dry food and water will suffice if you are away for only short periods. The amount of both will depend on the number of cats you have and the length of time you expect to be away. Or, to make sure they have a constant supply of fresh water, you might try one of those self-waterers that attach directly to the water faucet.

If you have several indoor cats, and they are all in good health and do not require extra meals or medication, you can safely leave them alone for a few days. Be advised though that they will show their indignation at being left alone by rearranging your house, so it is best to confine them to one area. Again, self-feeders for food and water are ideal. Make sure the water cannot spill (tip-proof water bowls are available as well as water-feeder containers), and be sure to leave extra litter pans.

Pet-sitters If you have kittens or older or sick cats needing extra meals and attention, it is best to have someone come in to care for them. Many neighborhoods have an exchange for pet-sitting. If an exchange is not possible, it's better to hire someone to pet-sit for you than to ask a friend or relative to do so. While they may be glad to help out in an emergency, if you make this a routine request and they do not take care of the cats properly, you have no recourse short of losing their

friendship should you complain.

In the more populated areas, you can find professional pet-sitters. They will come to your house once or twice a day, feed and water the cats, play with them and change their litter pan. Most pet-sitters will also bring in your mail and newspaper and water your indoor plants. Some even offer report cards on your cat.

Boarding If you can't arrange for a pet-sitter your only other alternative is to take your cat to stay with a friend or to board at a vet or boarding kennel. Neither of these options is a good idea. Cats dislike change and don't do well away from home. They show this by refusing to eat. A cat who doesn't eat is susceptible to becoming sick. And if you leave her

with a friend who has cats, she will not mix well with the other cats and so will have to be kept alone in a room. She will be prone to the same upsets as she is when boarded out and most likely will not eat.

water feeder

dry-food feeder

115

DE-SEXING/SPAYING

Unless you are a breeder, your cat will be far happier and make a better pet if she is neutered. This will also help reduce the number of unwanted cats, and probably save you a considerable sum of money in medical costs.

If left unaltered, your male cat will constantly howl, pace about and saturate your drapes and furniture with urine. The frustration of not siring (the indoor cat has no access to females) can also lead to severe weight loss, often resulting in illness. If you have a female cat, be aware that she can come in season as often as every few weeks throughout the entire year. She, too, will howl, pace and spray your furnishings.

Spaying Many females lose a large amount of weight when they are in season and may not have time to

AT THE VET
When a female kitten is spayed, the vet will remove her ovaries and uterus. This is a more involved operation than neutering a male (removing the testicles) and it will take her a few days to recover fully. Your vet will advise you on the best age to have your cat neutered. Generally though, a female can be spayed when she is only a few months old, but you should wait until a male is fully grown.

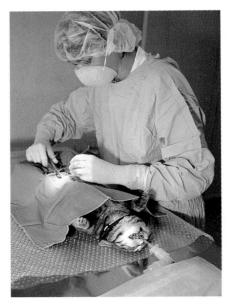

regain the weight before having another season. A female cat who has had even one litter of kittens runs a greater chance of contracting breast cancer than does the female who has been spayed without ever having had a litter. If you have a female who is not spayed, she is susceptible to uterine infections because of frequent seasons. One such infection, pyometra (see p. 136), can be fatal if not detected by the vet in time.

Some vets spay through a side incision, while others prefer the midline approach. Since shaving can cause permanent color changes, color pointed cats should always be operated on via a midline incision.

Neutering Although some people have no qualms about having a female spayed as they do not want her to have kittens, they may balk at having a male neutered. However, if your cat is to be kept completely indoors, it is cruel to leave him as an intact male and deny him access to normal mating with a female.

If you let him outdoors, you are responsible for contributing to the countless numbers of unwanted cats and kittens that are destroyed each year by humane societies worldwide.

The unaltered male also has a reflex action that comes into play if you stroke his tummy. As a kitten, he loves to roll over on his back and have you pet his tummy and tumble him over and over. As a fully mature male, however, if your petting hits just the right spot, he will—without warning—seize your hand with his hind legs and sink his teeth into it. He is not misbehaving—this is a purely reflex action.

The belief that an altered cat will become grossly overweight and no longer be a playful companion is not true. Because of hormonal changes occasioned by the neutering, he may not require as much food or may require food with a lower fat content. And, very often, he will revert to his kittenish self and become even more playful, since he will not be distracted by the mating urge. He will tend to give you much more affection than previously.

At what age? Your cat should be spayed or neutered at an appropriate age. Generally, it is thought that males need the male hormones for proper growth of their bones. Each cat differs as to his development but aside from the obvious signs of fully developed testicles, you will notice that his behavior has changed radically. Overnight, from being a frisky kitten he may turn into an aggressive male who plays too roughly with you and the other cats. This happens at around six to nine months and is a clear sign that it is time to have him neutered.

Females may be spayed when only a few months old. However, you should follow the advice of your vet as to the proper age for having your cat spayed or neutered.

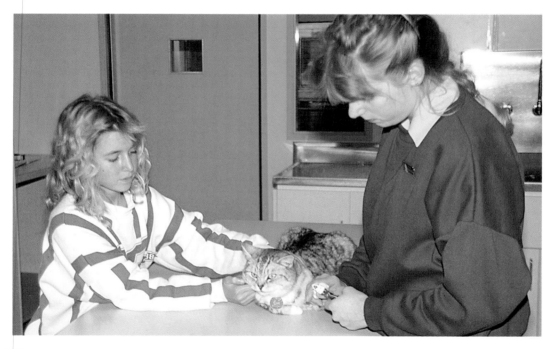

YOUR CAT'S HEALTH

The main requirements for your cat's health and happiness are that you keep a watchful eye on his comfort and safety, and provide plenty of food and love. He needs protection from environmental hazards, such as parasites and accidents, but just as most humans remain basically healthy, so will he. So don't be put off or overwhelmed by the following chapter. As with taking care of a small child, you need to be able to recognize potential problems so that if and when they occur, you can quickly take the appropriate steps. Regular veterinary check-ups will give you peace of mind and catch any illnesses that might occur before they become too serious.

A HEALTHY CAT

When stroking or grooming your cat, take the opportunity to look for any physical health problems. The earlier you detect symptoms, the easier it should be for your veterinarian to treat your cat successfully.

Warning signs Your cat keeps to a fairly regular routine, and so it should be easy to notice any of the many signs that could alert you to possible health problems. Signs to watch out for include:

• Change in everyday routine
• Listlessness

REGULAR CHECK-UPS
Make sure that you take your cat to the vet for his annual check-up. As well as picking up signs of illness early, your vet will see that any vaccination boosters are given when they're due.

• Behavioral changes
• Itchiness
• Excessive scratching
• Excessive cleaning
• Appearance of the third eyelid(s)
• Weight loss
• Decreased appetite
• Decreased thirst
• Drooling
• Limping
• Increased thirst
• Diarrhea
• Constipation
• Blood in feces
• Increased urination
• Straining while urinating
• Vomiting
• Bad breath
• Distended stomach
• Watery eyes
• Sneezing
• Coughing
• Dull coat
• Pale gums

• Take a look at your male cat's tail. If there is a build-up of a brown secretion and some swelling or hair loss around the base of his tail, he is suffering from stud tail.

• Gently feel your cat's body. If you feel any lumps and if his coat has lost its shine, he may be suffering from an abscess, particularly if he is a cat that goes outdoors. Or he may have a tumor. Most tumors detected will be benign, but it's best to have the vet check him.

• Gently pull the skin across his shoulders or back. If it stands out, or is slow to fall back into place, he may well be suffering from dehydration.

• Look inside your cat's ears to see if there is a dark brown waxy substance or any other sign of ear mites.

• Your cat's eyes should be clear and clean. The appearance of the third eyelid, or haw, is a sure sign that your cat is sick.

• Examine your cat's rear end. It should be clean and healthy. If there are signs of soreness, he may be suffering from diarrhea and if it persists, he should be taken to the vet.

• Carefully check inside your cat's mouth. His breath should be fresh and there should be no sign of tooth decay or gum disease.

• Is your cat not as agile as he used to be, and is he showing signs of stiffness in his joints? This may be nothing more than old age.

• Have you noticed your cat scratching himself more than usual, particularly around the head and rear? If so, he may be suffering from fleas or other parasites.

• To see if your cat is the proper weight, run your hands down his backbone and across his hip bones and lower abdomen. You should not be able to feel his bones easily.

• Look for cuts on your cat's paws or any damage to his nails. Do his claws need trimming?

THE BASICS

You can tell your cat is sick by watching his body language and looking for any variation in his everyday routine. Owners know their pets better than anyone else, so don't be afraid to follow your instinct if you think something is not quite right.

THIRD EYELID
The third eyelid, or haw, is a membrane in the corner of the eye nearest the nose. It is not visible in a healthy cat, but may appear when your cat is sick, partially covering the eye. It is either white or pink in color.

There are many signs that indicate your cat is unwell. If he is listless and does not greet you normally, if he stops eating his favorite food or if his normally sleek and shiny coat is dull and fluffed up, he is probably in distress. Other symptoms may include fever, a change in his normal behavior, or the appearance of the third eyelid, or haw.

Other signs of illness are more subtle and are harder to spot unless we pay careful attention. Does your normally outgoing female cat start hissing when you pick her up? This could be a sign of pain caused by a bladder problem. Does your shy and retiring older cat suddenly start attacking other cats even when not provoked? This, too, is a sign that something is wrong. The causes may range from nothing more than an infected tooth to a tumor.

And what about your three-month-old kitten? Has he stopped chasing his tail or pouncing on your toes under the covers? Has his appetite declined? If so, you should see these as alarm signals alerting you to take him to the vet. In a three-month-old it may be nothing more than normal teething, but it is best to have your vet check him.

Home care When your cat is ill, the most important thing you can do is keep him warm, quiet, well-fed and watered. Cats hate noise and bright lights and seek secluded areas when they are sick. For the indoor cat, set up a retreat in a room not used by members of your family or other pets. A soft towel lining a cardboard box and placed on the floor of a closet is ideal. With the door slightly ajar, the cat has darkness and solitude. For the outdoor cat, line a tire with an old blanket in the garage, making sure there are no drafts. To keep your cat warm, heating pads and hot water bottles are effective, and in extreme cases you can cut the foot off a sock or the sleeve off an old sweater to keep him warm.

In addition to following any medication prescribed, you need to supply your cat with plenty of fluids. If he will not drink water by himself, an eye dropper or plastic syringe can be used. If he clamps his teeth down firmly on the dropper and won't

DRINKING HELP
To prevent your sick cat from becoming dehydrated, see that he takes plenty of liquids. Gently insert a dropper filled with liquid into his mouth, and repeat regularly until he is drinking by himself again.

THE BASICS continued

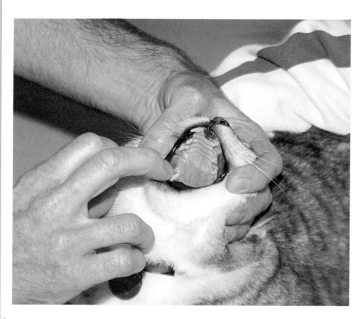

open his mouth, simply insert the tip through the side of his mouth. You will find an opening there and can squirt in the water. Clear chicken broth and the juices from either raw or cooked meat can also be used as fluids. Being slightly salty, these have the advantage of making your cat thirsty, prompting him to drink on his own initiative.

You should also ensure your cat eats enough, particularly if he has a cold. When cats have colds, they cannot smell. And when cats cannot smell, they do not eat. Place a small dab of food on your index finger and insert it in his mouth. Sometimes this is all it takes for his instinct to

OPEN WIDE
Indoor cats are much more likely to suffer from gum and dental problems than outdoor cats, so regularly check inside your cat's mouth and take him to the vet at the first sign of trouble.

take over. If it doesn't work, simply repeat the process. It is important to get him to eat; even the smallest amount will help him to recover.

If he still won't eat, there are products on the market that not only contain all the essential vitamins, minerals and amino acids, but the calories he needs as well. Try smearing one of these sticky supplements on your cat's front paws. Most cats cannot abide anything sticky on them and will lick it off. Or dissolve the supplement in hot water and use an eye dropper to give it to your cat as a liquid.

Cats hate to be dirty. When they are sick, they often fail to clean themselves thoroughly, so it is up to you to do it for them. Start with a soft cloth dampened with warm water. Gently clean his eyes and nose and around his mouth. Take a second cloth to clean his rear end because he may be too sick to do it himself after using the litter pan. Refrain from using soap or other

cleaning agents because you may cause allergic reactions or intensify the effects of the sickness. In severe cases, try brushing him gently or using a dry shampoo. Your soothing tone of voice and gentle hands will do wonders for his recovery.

DAILY ROUTINES
When cats are feeling well, they eat their food, use their litter pan and follow a fairly routine schedule of playing and sleeping. Any major change in this routine could signal a health problem.

VACCINATION

Many serious, even potentially fatal, illnesses can be prevented by vaccination. Some inoculations are compulsory while some are optional, but it is essential that you check with your vet for the best course of preventative medicine.

The "big three" All cats are susceptible to, and must be immunized against, three diseases—feline infectious enteritis (FIE) also known as panleukopenia, an often fatal infection of the intestines, causing loss of appetite, fever, vomiting and diarrhea; feline calicivirus (FCV), a severe strain of the common cold; and feline rhinotracheitis (FVR), also known as "cat flu." It is recommended that the vaccinations for these be given at 8 and 12 weeks of age, preferably using the modified live vaccine,

available in either injection form or nose drops. Exceptions to the above schedule are when you have an orphan kitten who is not building up immunities from his mother's milk, or if you have a large colony of cats and want them to be protected earlier.

Chlamydia After your kitten has received his two shots of what is commonly called the "three-in-one" vaccination (FIE, FCV and FVR), he will not require another vaccination until his annual checkup. At this

SYRINGE AND VACCINE VIAL
Vaccinations are carried out by your vet. Although they are normally given by injection, some may be given in the form of nose drops. Be sure you take your cat for his annual veterinary checkup. Not only will your vet give him any booster shots or vaccinations necessary, he will also check that your cat is not suffering from any diseases or ailments.

time, your vet may give him a booster shot comprising the three vaccines, and may also give him the chlamydia, or pneumonitis, vaccine. This immunizes cats against a number of strains of the common cold. It is strongly recommended that kittens under 12 weeks of age not be given the chlamydia vaccination as it can cause the kitten to come down with a severe cold, and in many cases they are left with chronic sinus conditions that will affect them for life. However, your cat should not experience any lasting side effects if he is immunized after 12 weeks.

FeLV, FIP and rabies The jury is still out on the advisability of giving vaccines for either the feline leukemia virus (FeLV), a complex and often fatal virus that attacks the bone marrow in kittens and can cause cancer; or feline infectious peritonitis (FIP), a disease that causes the lungs or abdomen to swell up with fluid. There is some concern that the FeLV vaccine can cause lumpy skin reactions that are called sarcomas. There is also some doubt as to whether the FIP vaccine is even effective.

The rabies vaccine should be given yearly to all cats that have any exposure to the outdoors. A cat that is never exposed to the outdoors will not require this vaccine.

You will need to check with your vet as to what treatments are available to cure some of the more common internal parasites, but these will not prevent the recurrence of the parasite.

It is also best to consult with your vet as to the best course of vaccinations for your particular cat or cats and the unique conditions in your household. For example, if you have a cat with a short nose and flat face, such as a Persian or an Exotic, who, due to reduced nasal capacity can be more prone to respiratory problems, your vet may choose to vaccinate earlier or more frequently. And the breeding queen, the male stud and the cat exhibited at shows may require more frequent boosters because they have a higher exposure to many diseases.

On the other hand, the single cat that is confined and living totally indoors may not require the same vaccinations as an outdoor cat or a cat from a multiple-cat household.

INTERNAL PARASITES

Most feline parasites live in the intestines of their host. While they are common among cats and are no cause for serious concern, you should take your cat to the vet if you suspect he is suffering from them.

whipworms

Roundworms These are a common parasite in cats that are either passed on from the mother or picked up by coming into contact with infected soil. They quickly multiply into large colonies and look like long strings of fine spaghetti. Adult roundworms live in the stomach and intestine. They can also survive in soil for years. The larvae hatch in the intestine and then move on to the lungs where they crawl up the windpipe and are swallowed, causing coughing. Although symptoms of infestation

roundworms

tapeworms

HOME DOCTORING
Worming paste can be given with a syringe (above left). If you have trouble administering prescribed pills, a pill-popper (right) may help.

are not always visible, they may include vomiting, diarrhea and a distended stomach.

All cats are susceptible to roundworms, but the greatest danger is to kittens who, if not treated, can die from a heavy infestation. Even if the mother is found to be free of roundworms, they may still be hidden in her body tissue. When she produces milk for her kittens, the worms come to life and infect the kittens via the mammary glands. Very often a check by the vet will not turn up any evidence of them because they

have not yet reached the intestines. So, take your kitten or cat to the vet 10 to 14 days after the first examination to make sure he is still free of them.

Tapeworm Another common parasite in cats is tapeworm, which feeds on the nutrients in the digestive tract. All that is visible to the naked eye is the segment, resembling a piece of rice, as it is broken off and

OUTDOOR LIFE
If your cat likes the great outdoors, there's not much you can do about a recurrence of parasites, but quick treatment will minimize damage.

SAFE, NOT SORRY
Little is known about heartworm in cats and the symptoms are vague. So, if your cat, like this Balinese, is feeling sick, and you think he could be susceptible to the disease, take him to see the vet immediately.

expelled through the anus. More often than not, there are no other visible symptoms.

The indoor cat can be infected with tapeworm through fleas, and the outdoor cat not only through fleas but also by eating mice or through infected soil and feces.

Your vet should first test for these parasites when your cat is three or four weeks of age, and prescribe the appropriate treatment, which will usually need to be repeated. Outdoor cats should be examined and treated by the vet twice a year as they will continually be exposed to the parasites. Indoor cats need to be checked only if you note any visible sign of the parasite.

Hookworms and whipworms
These are other internal parasites, but infestations are isolated and occur only in areas with a humid climate. Weakness, anemia, diarrhea and dermatitis are just some of the symptoms of hookworm. Unfortunately the symptoms of whipworm are less noticeable but include diarrhea and blood in the urine. Your vet will prescribe treatment, but the only preventative measure is to keep your cat indoors.

Toxoplasmosis This is an intestinal parasite contracted by most cats at some stage. But cats exhibit no symptoms, develop a natural immunity and are not threatened by the disease. Similarly, most humans have been exposed to toxoplasmosis, with the only symptom being a mild stomach upset. They, too, have developed immunities.

The danger of toxoplasmosis is to pregnant women as it can cause miscarriage and birth defects, but there is no danger if simple sanitary precautions are taken. For a pregnant woman to become infected, she would have to handle cat feces and then touch her mouth or nose with dirty hands. To avoid any possibility of danger, wear protective gloves when changing your cat's litter pan. A person could also catch the disease by handling raw meat and then eating without washing, or by eating meat that is not thoroughly cooked.

Coccidiosis Coccidiosis is a parasite found in feces. It can be contracted by your cat eating infected mice, birds or rabbits or through coming into contact with infected feces. If he is an indoor cat, he may have contracted the disease as a kitten in his previous home. Overcrowding of cat colonies or breeders' catteries coupled with poor sanitation contribute to the spread of this disease.

NURSING MOTHER
An infected queen can pass roundworms to her litter while nursing, even when the parasites have been dormant in her body.

If your cat is off his feed and has diarrhea, have him checked for coccidiosis. Aside from these symptoms, his feces will give off a strong, acrid odor and be gray in color. He may also suffer from listlessness, lack of energy and weight loss.

Strict hygiene and medication as prescribed by your vet can eradicate the problem in the indoor cat. The same treatment will apply to the outdoor cat, but eradication is almost impossible as his lifestyle is such that he will continue to be reinfected.

A combination of coccidiosis and roundworms can be fatal in kittens, so get prompt medical attention if you notice symptoms in your kitten.

FLEAS, TICKS AND MITES

External parasites live on the skin of your cat and feed on both his skin and blood, causing discomfort and, in some cases, minor sickness. They are a common problem for cats, particularly those that go outdoors, but your cat is easily treated and will recover quickly.

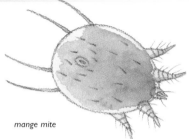

mange mite

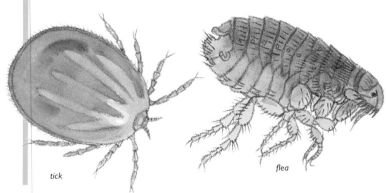

tick

flea

Fleas Many cats are highly sensitive to fleas. Some cats will react to the presence of a single flea not only by scratching vigorously but also by losing great patches of hair. Fleas tend to be more prevalent around the eyes, ears and anus, and your cat will scratch, suffer hair loss and become thoroughly miserable.

When combating fleas—and it is combat—you will need to give your cat repeated flea dippings as well as ridding his quarters and/or your living quarters of fleas. You must fumigate again within 10 to 14 days

after the first treatment as that is when the eggs hatch and a new crop of fleas emerges.

Some of the newer flea remedies include a monthly pill that is available only through your vet. Other remedies include flea collars, powders, sprays and baths. Do not combine a flea bath with any of the other flea remedies or you might poison your cat.

If you have indoor cats and a dog that goes outdoors into an enclosed yard, you can either hire a professional flea exterminator to spray your yard monthly, or you can purchase the equipment and do it yourself. If there are no fleas in the yard, the dog can't bring them into the house.

While it is not difficult to rid your indoor pet and your house of fleas, it

CAT SCRATCHING
Don't jump to conclusions just because your cat is scratching himself. All cats scratch and it does not necessarily mean that he is infested with parasites.

133

FLEAS, TICKS AND MITES continued

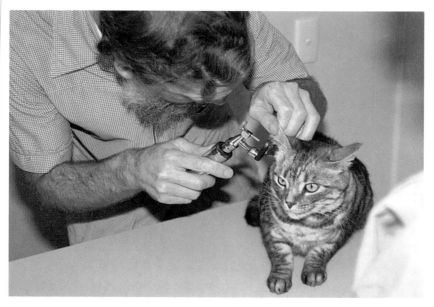

CHECK THE EARS
Take your cat to see the vet if you suspect he has ear mites. The vet will examine him and prescribe the appropriate treatment.

is impossible to rid the outdoor cat of them. The best you can do is follow your vet's advice and administer a prescription for treating the fleas.

Fleas not only carry tapeworm but can give your cat feline infectious anemia (FIA), a disease that can result in a low red blood cell count and a very sick cat. Symptoms include pale gums and a high temperature, but your vet will take a blood test to make a definite diagnosis, and will then prescribe the necessary treatment for your cat.

Ear mites For cats that socialize with others, ear mites are an occupational hazard. If you notice a dark brown waxy substance in your cat's ears, or if he torments himself by repeatedly scratching his ears, he may have ear mites. These are microscopic parasites that live in the ear canal and feed on skin and debris therein.

To make absolutely sure that ear mites are the problem, take your cat to the vet for examination and treatment. He will generally recommend the application of an oil-based liquid to eradicate them. You will probably need to repeat the treatment several times as these mites are persistent. In a multiple-cat household, the mites will quickly spread to all your cats. Your vet may prescribe enough medication to treat them all without examining them all.

As an alternative home treatment, dip a cotton swab into boric-acid powder, and gently clean the visible part of the inside of the ear only. The advantage of the dry powder is that it suffocates the mites and kills them, and may even discourage other mites from entering your cat's ears.

Ticks, head mites and mange

Ticks and mites are not often found on the indoor cat. If your indoor cat does have signs of any of these parasites, they have probably been carried in on dogs or human clothing. Outdoor and sick cats are most susceptible because they are more likely to be in contact with infected cats. If you detect a tick anywhere on your cat do not attempt to burn it off or pluck it out. A simple remedy is to cover it with petroleum jelly and leave it alone. The tick will die and fall off within a day or two.

Head mites are parasites that are not usually seen with the naked eye so if your cat is restless, itching or has lost his appetite, take him to the vet. Mites can also bring about mange, which can cause itchiness, dandruff and bald patches all over the cat's body. These symptoms can also be indicative of an allergic reaction or a hormonal change.

If you are concerned, you should take your cat to the vet, who might have to take a culture in order to prescribe treatment. Treatment for both mites and mange usually involves medicated baths at home. Although not a common problem among cats, once infected, outdoor cats will continue to be reinfected.

COMMON PROBLEMS

It is almost inevitable that your cat will, over the course of his life, become sick. Although most ailments are easily treated, some can be fatal, so it is important to be alert to any symptoms.

Pyometra This is an infection of the uterus that affects unaltered female cats. Symptoms may include listlessness, lack of appetite, great thirst and frequent urination, as well as a thick, creamy, odorous discharge from the vagina. However, some females exhibit no symptoms at all—your cat's coat may be shiny, her eyes clear and her appetite and behavior normal. Cats are so clean that you have to keep a close watch for any signs of vaginal discharge before she cleans it away.

However, there are signs to alert you to the increased possibility of pyometra. If your cat has frequent

FEEDING PROBLEMS
Keep a close watch for any changes in your cat's behavior. If your cat seems hungry as usual, yet eats only a small amount, he may have a sore mouth or an abscessed tooth. Check for obvious problems, but if the difficulty continues, ask your vet to check him.

seasons, or if her seasons are few and far between, she will be more susceptible to pyometra. Or if she has been mated, you may think she is pregnant when it is really the infection in the uterus causing her abdomen to appear plump with kittens.

The instant you spot the discharge take her to the vet. She can die if not treated immediately, as the infection can cause the uterus to burst. The most effective treatment for pyometra is a hysterectomy.

Feline Urological Syndrome (FUS) If your cat is having trouble urinating, if you see him straining in a squatting position or if there are traces of blood in his urine, take him to the vet at once. He could have feline urological syndrome (FUS), a lower urinary tract disease. This is a potentially fatal obstructive condition affecting one in five cats, usually mature and overweight males. Other symptoms include not using the litter pan, incontinence, frequent licking of the urinary area and great thirst. If not treated within 24 hours, your cat could die.

In addition to the vet unblocking the urethra and administering antibiotics, there is a surgical procedure if your cat suffers from repeated bouts. It is not known what causes FUS but it seems to run in bloodlines. Although there are no proven ways to prevent it from occurring, reducing the amount of dry food your cat eats may help.

Respiratory ailments Cats are more prone to respiratory problems than any other ailments. Although you have already protected your cat against the serious "cat flu," or FVR (see p. 126), he is still susceptible to around 100 other varieties of a cold. Even the chlamydia vaccine protects him against only some eight or nine varieties of the common cold.

Early symptoms of respiratory ailments include watery eyes, sneezing and coughing. You should take your cat to the vet as soon as these symptoms appear or nose and chest congestion may develop. Your vet may prescribe nose drops or a course of pills (be sure to finish the entire course; no stopping just because the symptoms seem to have gone away).

Although the vet will give the medication that is best for your cat's illness, it is up to you to provide the tender, loving care. Your cat will recover far more quickly at home than at the vet's, so be sure to follow the general care recommendations (see pp. 122–125), such as warming his food to blood temperature to tempt him to eat.

Allergies Cats are so prone to allergy that they can even become allergic to one another. Anything that might cause you to sniffle, cough,

137

COMMON PROBLEMS continued

wheeze or itch can have the same effect on your cat. In addition to external stimulants, cats can show allergic reactions to vaccinations, medications and even to some hormonal changes.

If you have just acquired a kitten, his immune system will still be developing, so you can expect him to show minor allergic reactions to your home. He may come from a home that has no carpet or upholstered furniture, so when he explores your home by sniffing the carpet and furniture he might sneeze or even cough until he develops immunities to the "fuzz" of the furniture or "nap" of the rug.

He may be allergic to your face powder or your perfume. And some cleaning agents, such as bleach and ammonia, should never be used near him unless diluted, and then only where there is proper ventilation and

the area can be thoroughly dried. If otherwise healthy, he should recover from allergic reactions within a few days to a week.

Many cats are allergic to flea preventatives or control remedies. And, if you use powder to help groom your longhaired cat, he may sneeze and his eyes may water just as yours might. At cat shows, by the end of the day, a walk down an aisle filled with longhaired cats is accompanied by the sounds of snorting and coughing and the sight of watering eyes, all because of the hair flying through the air and the various powders and sprays applied to the coats. In treating your cat, the vet may prescribe antihistamines.

Hand in hand with allergies is the possibility that your cat may develop asthma. You need your vet's help to control this to ensure that your pet lives a comfortable life.

Ringworm Scratching, biting and excessive washing of his coat can signal a number of different skin problems for your cat, including the stubborn condition of ringworm. Oddly enough, ringworm is not caused by a worm at all, but by a parasitic fungus.

It can be transmitted through contact with infected animals, soil or even humans. Kittens, pregnant queens and frail or elderly cats are most susceptible to the disease.

Signs of ringworm on your cat include a few broken hairs around the muzzle or ears as well as small, almost perfectly round, bald patches that later become crusty. Although most symptoms are found on the head, ears, paws and tail, they can appear anywhere on your cat's body. If you have an indoor/outdoor cat, or a multiple-cat household, you might mistake the first signs of ringworm for a scratch or bite on the ear inflicted by another cat.

If you suspect that your cat has ringworm, you should take him to the vet. The disease is easily treated by your vet with pills and/or injections. For an indoor cat, you should also vacuum the cat's living quarters and wash his bedding, toys and anything else that might harbor the fungus with a fungicide.

Since it is impossible to take these precautions with the indoor/outdoor cat or in totally outdoor cat colonies, there is no preventative for such cats.

Although some cats are carriers of ringworm, many develop natural immunities to the disease. Since the carriers do not show any symptoms, it is very difficult to track down and treat the cause of the recurring ringworm in your cats.

Cats can transmit ringworm to humans and dogs, and humans and dogs can transmit the disease to cats. If your cat is infected with ringworm, extreme care should be

WELL GERMS

When you introduce a new kitten or cat to your home, and you already have one or more cats, you should be aware that the new addition will not be immune to the "well germs" carried by your present cats.

Even though your other cats have received all of their shots and are in good health, they have become accustomed to the germs in your house and have built up immunities to them. Coming from another environment, your new cat is not immune to these germs and will more than likely come down with a respiratory infection or some other ailment within a week or two. Your other cats, in turn, have no immunities to the "well germs" of your new cat, so you can expect to encounter some minor illnesses in all your cats.

COMMON PROBLEMS continued

taken with him. If possible, isolate him until the scabs fall off the affected areas, taking with them the hairs that contain the spores.

Heartworm Feline Heartworm Disease (FHD) is rarely found in cats, but can be life-threatening. It is caused by parasites entering the bloodstream through the bite of an infected mosquito, and the parasites then migrate to the heart and pulmonary arteries where they mature and cause problems.

All cats are at risk, but those with increased exposure to mosquitoes are at highest risk. Warm, humid climates are ideal for transmission of heartworms. And don't think that your cat has to go outside to be bitten by mosquitoes. In fact, studies indicate that indoor cats may be hypersensitive to FHD infection. Unfortunately, the symptoms of FHD in cats are vague and differ markedly from the canine version. Researchers believe that cats with heartworms may be misdiagnosed with feline asthma, or may develop asthma as a consequence of FHD.

At present there is no definitive test for FHD in cats. Aside from asthma, other signs include weight loss, weakness and collapse. Although preventatives are well established for heartworm disease in dogs, there are none yet on the market for cats. There is a vaccine currently awaiting Food and Drug Administration approval in the US, that could be available in the near future.

Acne Surprisingly, cats can suffer from acne. It is generally found under the chin and around the mouth. This was originally called "Aby chin" because it was first diagnosed in the Abyssinian breed as it readily showed up on their white chins. Later it was learned that any cat can get acne.

It's a good idea to examine the chin area of your dark-colored cats to see if you can see or feel slight crusty bumps. These are easily seen on white or light-colored cats and look like coffee grains. Wash the affected area with a mild soap, rinse thoroughly with warm water and gently pat dry. Since acne thrives in damp places, you can help the drying process by rubbing cornstarch on light-colored cats or Fuller's earth on dark ones.

Causes of acne can range from eating from plastic dishes to food becoming embedded in the chin. Since cats continue to eat, the possibility of them having acne is ongoing, but a careful check of the chin and weekly washings can keep your cat pimple-free.

Abscesses Abscesses are hidden dangers. Often, we cannot see them, but we can feel them. If your cat shows no external sign of a wound, but is listless, off his eating schedule, has a dry, open coat or is not acting normally, there is a chance that he could be suffering an infection from an abscess.

This is a tricky and often deadly situation because the skin will close over an open wound, leaving no visible sign. If your fingers do detect a lump anywhere on your cat, it could be an abscess. To treat, soak a cloth in hot water (not so hot that it will burn the skin) and then soak the infected area. The hot water serves to draw out the pus in the abscess and it will seep through a tiny opening in the skin if you apply a gentle squeezing action.

After you have extracted as much pus as possible, wash the area with warm water and apply hydrogen peroxide with a cotton ball. The abscess needs to drain so do not

bandage the area. If this process doesn't relieve the cat within three or four days, take him to the vet. An untreated abscess can lead to blood poisoning.

Stud tail Stud tail is so called because it is generally found in the unaltered tomcat, although it can affect females. It is the build-up of a brown secretion caused by the release of oils from the gland on the upper surface of the cat's tail, near the base. You will also notice swelling, blistering and hair loss in this area.

This condition can be controlled easily by washing and completely drying the affected area on a regular basis. If the skin is red and sore, your vet may prescribe a balm that can be applied to relieve irritation.

As long as your cat remains unaltered, he will continue to secrete excessive oil from the glands at the base of the tail so vigilance is necessary to keep him comfortable.

Dandruff Just like you, your cat may develop dandruff, and for just about as many reasons. If he is light-colored, you may not notice the dandruff, but if his coat is dark, you will be able to see the dandruff clearly. In either case, simply petting or brushing him will bring the dandruff to the surface.

Don't panic if you see a small amount of dandruff. This is normal because the skin changes and is shed periodically. However, if the condition is severe, have him checked by your vet. The reason could be diet, a lack of oil or a skin or a parasitic condition.

Altered cats and older cats have more dandruff than unaltered and younger ones. When a cat is altered, he will suddenly be lacking the hormones that help promote a healthy skin and coat. Your vet may be able to prescribe medication or dietary supplements to make up for this deficiency. The natural process of aging will probably cause your cat

COMMON PROBLEMS continued

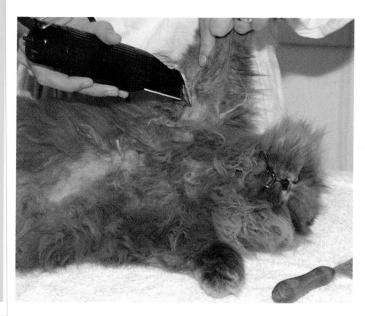

to gradually develop a thicker and drier coat and scaly skin, which might cause more dandruff. Again, a dietary supplement and an occasional bath will help. You will probably not be able to cure the dandruff completely but you will be able to control it.

Wool-chewing Some cats are wool-chewers. This is a loose description that encompasses cats who not only chew wool but chew towels, socks and blankets as well. Most chewers are either Siamese, part-Siamese or Burmese and they start chewing as soon as they have

TREATING MATTED FUR

If your longhaired cat's coat becomes seriously matted, you may have to call on the help of a professional groomer to clip away the tangles. Your vet may even have to sedate the cat. With regular grooming, things should not reach such a sorry pass.

teeth. The easiest solution is to remove the temptation either by putting these possessions away or by not letting your cat into areas where they are kept. It is just about impossible to stop a wool-chewer from chewing.

And sometimes he will chew on himself! Some cats, and not just Siamese, suck on their tails much like a baby sucks on his thumb. He may also nurse on himself or other adult cats. You can break him of this habit by applying a bitter tasting liquid to his tail and other areas where he chews. If you let him chew on his tail unchecked, he could cause such mutilation that part of the tail is eventually chewed off.

Spraying Spraying is a natural instinct whereby cats squirt strong-smelling urine on vertical surfaces, generally to mark territory. It is most common in the unaltered male who will spray to attract females and warn off other tomcats. Unaltered females spray to a lesser extent, usually to attract tomcats. There is really nothing that you can do to stop an unaltered cat from spraying.

A neutered male or a spayed female will also spray on occasion, but not for the same reasons as an unaltered cat. If you move, change your routine or go on vacation, your altered pet may show his petulance by spraying on your furniture. Other things that might induce him to spray are the mating seasons—spring and fall—when he can hear and smell the unaltered males and females mating.

Another common reason altered cats spray is because you have acquired one cat too many, or one of your cats has a new litter of kittens. They spray to tell you that they are unhappy. This is an instinctive response on their part and they should not be punished. They will stop spraying when the kittens go to their new homes, or when, in time, they have accepted the new cat.

Shedding While outdoor cats shed twice a year, indoor cats may shed hair for the entire year. This is due to the fairly consistent temperature and lighting found inside the house. Older cats tend to shed more than younger ones because they usually have a drier coat.

If you suspect that your cat is shedding excessively, you should take him to the vet. If no illness is diagnosed, the shedding may be caused by a hormonal imbalance or by a lack of some nutrients in his diet. Most likely, though, it is caused by illness, skin allergy or parasites. Daily combing and brushing, combined with hand-grooming and an occasional bath, will help to control the problem.

Hairballs If your cat has lost his appetite and has constipation and bowel problems, he could be suffering from hairballs. These are formed by your cat swallowing hair while cleaning and grooming

COMMON PROBLEMS continued

himself. The hair forms into cylindrical shapes in the intestine, and these are often vomited up.

Most cats will choose your best chair, your bed or the living-room rug to relieve themselves of a hairball, having held on to it while passing a perfectly acceptable tiled floor. Why he won't use the bare floor to vomit is a mystery. One theory suggests that he doesn't want the hairball mixture to splash up in his face or stand out prominently. There is a strong instinct that even the indoor cat has to "hide" his waste from predators.

The indoor cat will often use dry food as an emetic. You might see him work his way through a portion of dry food and, within a minute, vomit up a perfectly formed roll that also contains hair. The outdoor cat and indoor/outdoor cat will vomit up the hairball after eating grass.

Daily combing combined with the occasional bath can aid in controlling hairballs. There are also hairball remedies on the market that you can administer to your cat on a weekly basis. These help the cat eliminate any hairballs by lubricating the intestines, thereby allowing the easy passage of the hairball.

However, if the hairball has become impacted in his intestines, you might need to take your cat to the vet to have the hairball removed surgically under an anesthetic.

Whisker problems Whiskers are very important to your cat. He uses them as feelers to avoid bumping into things in the dark, to measure the width of a space to ensure that he will fit through, and when he is out hunting.

Whiskers can also be a bother to him, especially if he tries to eat food from a bowl. The ends of the whiskers touching the side of the bowl transfer irritating sensations to his brain, making it hard for him to continue eating. It's rather like you eating while your head is encased in a bag—the sides of the bag rubbing against your face wouldn't make for an enjoyable meal.

Whiskers are extremely sensitive because they are closely connected to the nervous system. Any damage to his whiskers will cause your cat discomfort, and he may become confused or disoriented. Don't ever trim his whiskers, and don't ever wash them—he will keep them perfectly clean by himself.

When he was a kitten, his mother might have chewed some or all of his whiskers off while cleaning food from them. Don't worry—this is absolutely normal and they will soon grow back again.

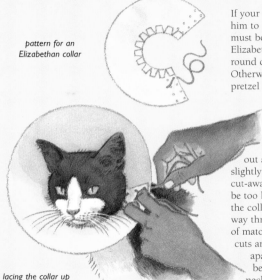

pattern for an Elizabethan collar

lacing the collar up

ELIZABETHAN COLLAR

If your cat is recovering from surgery and you don't want him to pull out his stitches, or if he has a wound that must be kept bandaged, you will need to fit him with an Elizabethan collar (so called because it looks like the round collars worn by women in the Elizabethan age). Otherwise, you will find that he can contort himself like a pretzel to reach every location on his body and will work steadily until he succeeds in removing the offending stitches or bandages.

Your vet will provide you with such a collar or you can make one yourself. Simply take a sturdy but flexible material, such as cardboard, and cut out a circle. Cut out a smaller circle in the center, slightly larger than the size of his neck to allow for the cut-away portion (see illustration). The collar should not be too loose or he will slip his head through and remove the collar. Cut away about a quarter of the circle all the way through to the center opening. Punch a double row of matching holes on either side of the gap. Make short cuts around the inner circle about ½ inch (1.25 cm) apart and bend back flaps. These allow the edge to bend for a snug fit. Place the collar around your cat's neck and use string to lace the open sides together.

ADMINISTERING MEDICINE

Sharp teeth and claws make administering medicine to a cat a hazardous operation. If possible, recruit someone to help you by holding the animal firmly. Some professionals suggest wrapping the cat in a thick towel to keep the paws out of the way.

ADMINISTERING NOSE DROPS
Hold your cat gently but firmly while you administer nose drops. Then continue to hold his head in a tilted position until you are sure the drops are well inside the nasal passages. He will almost always sneeze after having nose drops, so stand clear.

ADMINISTERING EAR DROPS
Your cat could suffer from an ear infection caused by a variety of bacteria and fungi. Apply the drops into his ear as instructed by your vet, then gently massage the base of his ear for a few seconds.

OPEN WIDE
Open your cat's mouth by placing one hand on the cheek bones of his upper jaw and then pushing his lower jaw open with your other hand.

Popping a pill Now we face the difficult chore of giving your cat a pill. By following the steps outlined, it will be easier for both of you.

If your cat struggles, have someone else hold him while you insert the pill. As a last resort, try wrapping him in a blanket, but be careful as he may struggle even more. Some cats will never let you open their mouth, so if your cat objects, mash the pill with a spoon. It can then be mixed either with water, broth or food.

If your cat doesn't swallow the pill, gently pinch the skin on his throat and pull it outward. This will open up the passageway so the pill can more easily slip down.

INSERTING THE PILL
Using a pill-popper or the fingers of your lower hand, insert the pill well back in the mouth. Close the mouth and stroke the throat to encourage him to swallow.

STROKING THE THROAT
Gently stroking your cat's throat will encourage him to swallow. Once you have seen him lick his nose, you can be almost certain that he has swallowed.

ADMINISTERING MEDICINE continued

Administering eye medication

If possible, have someone else hold the cat securely (see p. 72–73). With your thumb, pull either the top lid up (see below) or the lower lid down and lay a strip of ointment along inside the full length of the lid. Release the eyelid. When it closes, the ointment will soften and form a film over the eyeball and the conjunctiva.

For eye drops, tilt the head back. With the thumb and index finger of one hand, hold the eyelids apart gently and drop the drops onto the eyeball. Keep holding the head, tilted, for about 20 seconds or the drops will roll out and be wasted.

ADMINISTERING EYE DROPS
After applying ointment or liquid to your cat's eyes, hold him loosely for a few moments to let the medication do its job; otherwise, your cat will immediately rub it out.

WHEN ACCIDENTS HAPPEN

Every household with pets should have a first-aid kit in case of emergencies. It should include all the items at right. When you are away from home with your cat, you will also need the following items: carrying cage, muzzle, collar and leash, bowl for washing wounds, towel or blanket, tourniquet and sheeting for binding wounds.

• Approach an injured cat with caution; he will be very frightened and likely to bite and scratch.

• Try to calm him by talking quietly and, if there are no signs of aggression, stroking, but don't touch the injured area.

• If the cat seems cold, or if he is so frightened that he scratches you as you approach, cover him with a light rug or towel.

• If the cat is rushing about in panic, try to confine him to a small space. If he is not moving see that he is in a comfortable position.

See the following pages for how to deal with specific emergencies.

FIRST-AID KIT

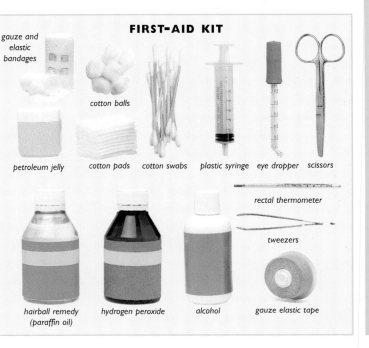

gauze and elastic bandages

cotton balls

petroleum jelly   cotton pads   cotton swabs   plastic syringe   eye dropper   scissors

rectal thermometer

tweezers

hairball remedy
(paraffin oil)   hydrogen peroxide   alcohol   gauze elastic tape

TREATING INJURY AND ILLNESS

It's easy to say that if an accident occurs, you should take your cat to the vet. But what if the vet's office is closed? Or what if you live hundreds of miles away from the vet? Here are some of the things you'll need to know.

Accidents will happen, and the best way to handle them is to be prepared. Make sure you have a properly equipped first-aid kit (see previous page), be aware of the types of injuries your cat might suffer, and know how best to treat them.

Some treatments are straightforward—if your cat is choking, you may be able to remove the obstruction from his throat with tweezers. Other accidents, however, require more complex treatment, and this easy-reference section will explain how you can best treat your cat in an emergency.

APPLYING PRESSURE

If your cat is bleeding, apply a pressure bandage to the wound. If the bleeding continues, you may need to apply a tourniquet between the wound and the heart and take him quickly to the vet for treatment.

Bleeding The main point of bleeding will be where your cat is licking. Although most bleeding will stop of its own accord, if your cat is bleeding heavily you will need to apply either a pressure bandage or a tourniquet.

A pressure bandage, which stops the blood flowing at the wound, is used when the bleeding is not too severe. Apply a cold-water compress onto the wound and then put on a pressure bandage of gauze and fasten with tape or torn sheeting.

If your cat is bleeding profusely, you may need to use a tourniquet, which stops the blood flowing to the wound. To apply, bind a strip of cloth tightly above the wound and release it every few minutes to let the blood flow for a second or two. Then

FRACTURES FROM JUMPING
Your cat will not always land on his feet, and may suffer a fracture in a bad landing. Never try to splint his leg yourself, it's a job for a professional. Take him to the vet.

bind it tightly again and repeat the process until the bleeding stops or you can get to your vet's office.

If blood is coming from your cat's nose or some other inaccessible area, apply an ice pack and keep him very still. If his tail is bleeding, wrap a pressure bandage around the wound. Use only tape or torn sheeting to fasten bandages on a cat, never pins.

Fractures If your cat has fallen from a height or is struck by a car and you can readily see that he has a fractured leg, the most important thing is to prevent him from going into shock or to minimize the effects of shock. Cover him lightly, keep him warm, talk to him in low tones and a soothing manner, and do not rush. Lift him as carefully as possible

so as not to worsen any damage, place him in a small container and take him to the vet immediately. Only a vet can splint an injured limb and, most often, only under anesthesia. Although you might want to try to splint the limb, bear in mind that most cats do not tolerate being handled when they are in pain and your best efforts will probably be greeted by teeth flashing and claws striking. You may well cause even more damage.

Burns Your cat could suffer serious injury if he jumps on a hot stove or tips over a pan of boiling water. If it is a superficial burn or scald, the affected area turns red and could blister slightly. If the burn is more serious, the skin will turn white and the hairs will pull out easily. To treat, immediately apply cold water

TREATING BURNS
To treat burns, immediately cool the area by applying cold water or ice. Small packets of frozen vegetables make excellent ice packs in an emergency.

or ice to the affected area for about 20 minutes. If the burn is serious, you will need to take your cat to the vet for further treatment. Otherwise, you will just have to let nature take its course.

You can help prevent these accidents by keeping pans away from the edge of the stove and by covering gas and electric rings with fireproof lids. Kitchens can be the heart of the home, and very much your cat's domain. When you allow him access to this area, you must take the necessary precautions.

Electrocution Many cats, especially kittens, will chew on wires. Some even like to chew on wire coat hangers. With today's electrical equipment, it's almost impossible not to have wires lying about your house.

If your cat has been electrocuted, don't touch him until you have turned off the power and removed the plug from the socket. Check for his heartbeat by feeling the lower part of his chest just behind the left foreleg. If he is unconscious, you may need to rush him to the vet for treatment. Never attempt to resuscitate him yourself.

If the shock is not sufficient to render him senseless, it can still inflict a serious burn on his tongue or in his mouth. Take him to the vet as soon as you can to avoid any possibility of gangrene setting in.

To protect your cat from any further electrocution, make an effort to unplug all appliances when you're not using them.

Drowning Although they may be very good swimmers, cats, just like people, can drown, particularly if they fall into a swimming pool. Even a toilet bowl can be hazardous to a kitten. Cats cannot climb over a ledge to get out of water, so unless there is help at hand, the incident could be fatal.

If your cat is drowning, remove him from the water as quickly as possible. Then, holding him by his hind legs, swing him gently between your legs until all the water has been expelled.

Fever When your cat is feeling listless and not eating or drinking, he may have a high temperature. Gently pinch the skin over the shoulders; if it doesn't snap back immediately, he is probably becoming dehydrated.

To take his temperature, coat the bulb of a rectal thermometer with petroleum jelly. Gently, using a slow, twisting motion, insert it about one inch (2.5 cm) into his rectum, and leave it for one minute, all the time holding the base of the tail firmly.

A cat's normal temperature is 101° F (38° C). If your cat is running a fever, take him to the vet at once. Never give him aspirin or any other drug made for humans as they can be fatal to cats.

Vomiting It is not unusual for your cat to vomit, and he may be doing nothing more than ridding himself of a hairball (see p. 143). Similarly, if your cat is vomiting only after meals, he may simply be overeating. Try putting a smaller amount of food in his bowl. Or if yours is a multi-cat household, make sure he has his own food bowl or feed him in a separate place. Your cats may be competing for food and therefore eating too quickly.

If the vomiting continues, your cat may be allergic to certain foods. Stop feeding him for 12 hours, but be sure to encourage him to drink plenty of water to avoid him becoming dehydrated. Then give him only bland foods (available from your vet) for the next 24 hours. If everything seems fine, slowly reintroduce variety into his diet and you should, given time, discover his allergy.

Whenever your cat's vomiting is combined with not eating, not drinking, or not behaving in his usual manner, or if there are signs of blood in his vomit, you should take him straight to the vet. This could signal one of many more serious illnesses, including poisoning, gastritis, ulcers, allergic reactions to insect bites or even feline infectious enteritis (FIE) (see p. 126).

Up in a tree One day you may find your cat stuck in a tree, and neither one of you will know what to do. In most cases, when he feels hungry, he will make his own way down. But sometimes, if he is sick or panicked, he will be too frightened to come down and you will need to step in. Try calling and coaxing him, or lure him within reach by offering his favorite food.

If these methods fail, then it's time for more drastic measures. Call your neighborhood fire department and ask for help. If they can't come, cover yourself with a long-sleeved shirt and put on thick gloves (your cat will probably scratch and may even try to bite you). Take along a small towel; if you can cover him with that you have a better chance of catching him.

Get a ladder and stay very calm because if he becomes any more frightened, he may climb even higher up the tree. If all attempts at rescue fail, all you can do is leave food as close to him as possible.

CLIMBING TREES
Cats love to climb about in trees, but they sometimes get stuck and seem unable to get down. Tempting them with food may provide an incentive to try harder,

POISONS

Your curious cat will want to investigate every corner of his territory. A cupboard with an open door is irresistible to him, so take the same precautions as you would with a toddler and keep household cleaners and gardening products out of reach in locked cupboards.

Poisoning Most household products that are poisonous to humans will also be poisonous to your cat. Make sure you keep all your household cleaners and other such toxic substances well out of harm's way. Even antifreeze in your car could be fatal to your outdoor cat if he licks up drops of it from underneath the car.

If you think your cat has been poisoned, try to ascertain what the poison is. If it is not corrosive, as a first-aid measure induce vomiting by dosing him with water mixed with either salt or bicarbonate of soda (baking soda). If it is corrosive, don't induce vomiting, and in either event, immediately take him to be checked by your vet.

SNIFFING CATNIP

Catnip (*Nepeta cataria*) has a strange effect on cats and they love to roll on the plant or rub against it. It is harmless.

clematis

yew

poinsettia

delphinium

POISONOUS PLANTS

The indoor cat is exposed to just about as many toxic substances as the outdoor one. We often forget that the thriving philodendron plant or blooming wisteria can be toxic to him, so here is a list of some of the common indoor and outdoor plants that are potentially dangerous to your cat.

Anemone	Four o'Clock	Mountain Laurel
Azalea	Hellebore	Oleander
Black Cherry	Hemlock	Philodendron
Bloodroot	Holly	Poinciana
Buttercup	Hyacinth	Poinsettia
Caladium	Hydrangea	Poison Ivy
Castor Bean	Indian Spurge Tree	Poison Oak
Clematis	Jack-in-the-pulpit	Pokeweed
Crocus	Jerusalem Cherry	Rhododendron
Cycad	Jimson Weed	Solandra
Daphne	Lantana	Star of Bethlehem
Delphinium	Larkspur	Sweet Pea
Dicentra	Liburnum	Thornapple
Dieffenbachia	Lily-of-the-valley	Wisteria
Elephant's Ear	Lupin	Yew
English Ivy	Mistletoe	
Foxglove	Morning Glory	

OLDER CATS

Your cat has been with you for many years, and you have learned to trust each other. Don't let him down now. As he enters old age, you must pay even greater attention to his needs and provide plenty of tender loving care.

CARING FOR THE ELDERLY
Gently groom your aging cat every day, even if he is shorthaired. As you comb him, run your fingers lightly over his body to see if he is developing tumors. Many old-age tumors are benign, but it's best to have a vet check them out, just in case.

Life expectancy With improved diets and advances in medicine, cats, just like humans, are living longer. However, old age can vary dramatically from one cat to another. A strictly indoors cat with a good diet and regular vaccinations will probably outlive an outdoor cat, an indoor/outdoor cat and a feral cat. It is not uncommon for indoor cats to live up to 18 years or more. Outdoor cats, on the other hand, generally live to about 15 years, although many may die much sooner and others live to more than 20 years.

Signs of old age You can tell if your cat is entering old age when he does not jump onto his favorite perches easily, or at all. He will sleep more, and when awake, he will move slowly and with a hint of stiffness. However, he will not be as prone to arthritis and backaches as dogs, and should remain agile for a long time.

Although you may not notice at first because he is adept at keeping to a routine, your cat may start to lose his hearing and eyesight. It's a good idea to let him see your hand in front of his face before you pick him up, and to call his name before you approach him.

He may also start to develop problems with incontinence, diarrhea and constipation. Sometimes these are caused by kidney problems or

GENERAL DECLINE
As he grows older, your cat may sleep more and pay less attention to his careful grooming routine. He needs extra kindness and gentle handling.

diabetes, but usually they are simply part of the aging process.

For incontinence and diarrhea, you will need to take him to the vet to determine the cause, and then follow the prescribed treatment. If he has a constipation problem, your vet can recommend a supplement, such as a stool softener, and he may suggest including more oils in your cat's diet. Do not add oil unless you've discussed the type and quantity of oil with the vet. Many common oils will deplete your cat's natural supply of essential vitamins.

Drooling and bad breath are a sure signal to take your elderly cat to the vet. It could be nothing more than a gum infection or a decayed tooth that needs extracting, or it may

PEACEFUL END
Sometimes the kindest thing you can do for an old, sick cat is to have him put to sleep humanely by your vet.

signify something more serious. Don't worry if he has to have his teeth extracted. Many cats continue to eat their normal food—and even crunch dry cat food—with no teeth at all. Their hardened gums will take over the job quite effectively.

The outdoor or aging farm cat may develop irritating skin conditions so you will need to watch him carefully and help him maintain a clean coat. He may also harbor maggots that feast on damp and dirty skin that results from fecal staining. An indoor/outdoor or totally indoor cat who is properly cared for will not be troubled by maggots.

Weight and diet Pay special attention to your elderly cat's weight. As he ages, obesity will exacerbate any difficulties he may have breathing, or even moving about.

You might be deceived into thinking he is too thin because his flesh will start to sag from his backbone and the vertebrae will be more prominent. This is perfectly normal and doesn't mean that he is underweight.

As a general rule, you should feed him less as he ages or, if he really loves to eat, you might try a diet lower in fats and proteins.

Euthanasia When your cat can no longer eat or drink on his own, and has lost the will to engage in his normal pastimes, it is time to think about doing the kindest thing you can for him and that is euthanasia.

The completely outdoor cat and the feral cat will remove themselves from their colony and creep off somewhere to die. However, your indoor cat doesn't have this option.

The decision to have him humanely euthanized is difficult. Not only are you contemplating the loss of your trusted friend, but you could suffer feelings of guilt. Just remember you are truly doing the right thing in putting an end to his misery and suffering in the kindest possible way.

YOUR CAT'S AGE IN HUMAN YEARS

When your cat is one year old, he is a similar age to a 20-year-old human. For each year after, simply add four humans years to every one of his. For example, if he is 15 years old in cat years, he is 76 years old in human years, with all the aches, pains and stiffness in his joints that accompany that age. The chart will help you calculate the age of your cat:

CAT	HUMAN
1 YEAR	20 YEARS
2 YEARS	24 YEARS
3 YEARS	28 YEARS
4 YEARS	32 YEARS
5 YEARS	36 YEARS
6 YEARS	40 YEARS
7 YEARS	44 YEARS
8 YEARS	48 YEARS
9 YEARS	52 YEARS
10 YEARS	56 YEARS

CAT BEHAVIOR

Cats communicate with one another using facial expression, body postures and vocalizations. Humans can learn to understand some of these exchanges, but many are very subtle and not meant for us. Not all behaviors are purely instinctive. Hunting, for example, is learned by observing the mother and practicing the various skills with siblings. Your cat will easily learn other skills, too, as long as there is something in it for him. If you want to train him, try food rewards until he gets the idea, but reduce the amount you feed him at mealtime so that he doesn't get too fat. You will need plenty of patience, because cats sleep a lot and will cooperate only when they are in the mood.

BODY LANGUAGE

As you get to know your cat, you will begin to understand quite clearly what he says with his voice and every part of his body. Unlike humans, cats never mask their feelings but are always honest and open. Just remember, though, that the main purpose of his body language is to communicate with other cats, not with you.

HISSING
When confronting a perceived threat, your cat's first reaction will be to draw back and hiss. If the threat continues, he will choose either to flee the scene or move into full fight mode with fluffed-up coat and tail, and low growling.

Hoisting a flag Your cat's tail gives a good indication of his mood. An angry cat swishes his tail from side to side and growls aggressively while deciding how to proceed. On the other hand, a tail raised straight and high tells you that he's happy and relaxed. As the tail position lowers, so does the mood. A horizontal tail may mean that he is stressed or unsure of himself, and if it drags along the ground he may be unhappy or even sick.

Vocalizing The range of meows your cat utters will convey his meaning clearly as you become more familiar with his ways. Some breeds are more vocal than others, with Siamese cats being notorious for the piercing wails they emit at night. These can be mistaken for a human baby in great distress, but are perfectly normal for this breed.

Cats learn quickly that owners respond well to meows and purring. As well as attention, it often gets them food. As vocal interactions continue, the bond between owner and cat is strengthened.

Purring We are not sure why cats purr, but it seems to keep his air sacs open during shallow breathing, to express pleasure, and to have a calming effect on the purrer. Kittens purr in response to their mother's attentions and when they are suckling, but a queen may also purr during labor and some cats purr even in the face of pain and aggression. Humans respond very positively to a purring cat, so it's an effective way of getting attention.

Kneading When a kitten kneads the mother's nipple area to release milk, it is deeply content, receiving all it needs at that moment. An older cat that continues this behavior when he sits in total security on your lap may be revisiting the happiness of that time.

Meeting and greeting When two friendly cats meet, they touch noses, sniffing each other's body from face to anus. This is their way of gathering information about each other. Should your cat greet you by sniffing at your nose and face in similar fashion, you can take it as a compliment, but you don't have to sniff him back.

During the greeting and follow-up examination, the necks of both are stretched out and their bodies are slightly crouched. The encounter looks quite wary and tentative and if one cat is more dominant than the other he will crouch lower in a rather submissive way and turn his body slightly away.

When two unfriendly cats have an encounter, it's a different story. They will hiss and stare each other down. They may fluff themselves up, or one may even turn side-on to the other in order to appear larger.

Submission When a confrontaton between two cats takes place, one will usually back down, crouching low and flattening his ears until they are almost invisible from the front. The pupils are dilated and the submissive cat may slink away or even roll over onto his back. By submitting, the cat avoids having the confrontation escalate into a fight and so escapes without injury.

The Flehmen Response This peculiar grimace is thought to help the cat to detect subtle odors. The

BODY LANGUAGE continued

lips are curled back, the nose wrinkled and the mouth open as the cat breathes in, tasting and smelling the air with the help of a special organ in the roof of the mouth called Jacobson's organ. The cat is said to be "flehming". In the domestic cat, this facial expression is usually observed on a male that is checking out the breeding readiness of a female. The Flehmen response is more easily observed in larger members of the cat family, say at your nearest zoo.

Ears Your cat's ears move to catch interesting sounds, but their position also conveys messages to other cats. When threatened or angry, your cat will flatten his ears and pull them down sideways. To send an invitation to play, he will pull them down and back.

Eyes When your cat is angry, excited or frightened, you will notice that his pupils become dilated. As he relaxes again the pupils contract to mere slits. When he is alert or anxious his blinking will be rapid. When all's right with the world and life returns to its customary slow pace, his blinking will slow down, too.

During a confrontation with another cat, or while preparing to attack prey, your cat will seem not to blink at all. His stare is steady and unwavering. When two cats do this to each other, one eventually will decide to back down and leave the scene quietly.

STEADY GAZE
Eyes fixed, pupils narrowed to slits and ears forward to catch every sound, this cat is assessing what is moving about among the leaves in his owner's garden.

BODY LANGUAGE continued

STANDING
This cat is focused on some toy or object his owner is using to hold the cat's attention. All his hunting instincts are on full alert and this is a game he never tires of playing.

Body posture A fluffed-up tail and arched back are clear signs that your cat is threatened and afraid. If his aggressor is a dog, the bushy tail will be vertical as he hisses, growls and spits while deciding what to do next. If the aggressor is hesitant, your cat may attack, regardless of the size of the dog. If the dog holds his ground, your cat may take the sensible option and flee.

In stalking mode, your cat holds his body close to the ground as he creeps forward with tail down. If your cat is upset with you, he may turn his back and ignore you to show his displeasure.

Lordosis posture Female cats in estrus often assume an unmistakable posture: front end down, back end up with the hindlegs bent and knees close to the ground. The tail is swept to one side and the back feet paddle furiously. Novice owners sometimes think that their pet has been hurt in

DEMANDING ATTENTION
This pose is one some owners see almost every day at meal times. Meowing to get your attention, your cat will walk around your feet, rubbing his body against your legs until you pay attention and give him what he wants: his dinner.

an accident and call their vet in panic. After a few relevant questions, the vet can explain what is going on and reassure the owner.

Signaling with feces When your cat defecates on his own territory, he will usually cover his stool, or at least attempt to. Away from home, however, he may leave it exposed as a signal to others that he has been there. This may be what is happening when he defecates in an inappropriate place in the house. He's reminding you that he is there.

Leg rubbing There's no mistaking the message that your cat is pleased to see you when he rubs himself against your legs, his tail held high.

MORE THAN A WARM WELCOME
This cat is certainly pleased to greet his owner, and is signaling affection and acceptance. But he is also affirming his relationship with this important human by marking his owner's pants with scent from his sebaceous glands.

AGGRESSION AND FIGHTING

While cats tend to avoid fighting whenever possible, there are some cases where it is the only way to retain their rights and standing in the cat hierarchy. Unfortunately, the loser risks getting bitten, often on the tail, as he beats a hasty retreat.

A STANDOFF
Unexpected meetings result in raised hackles and a great deal of staring and hissing, with both cats trying to hold their ground. Eventually, one will back down and leave, probably pretending that he didn't want to be there anyway.

Body signals Cats use combinations and gradations of facial expression, body postures and vocalizations to communicate with one another. Nowhere is this better demonstrated than during aggressive exchanges. Gradations of facial expressions include altering the size of the pupils and, more important, changing the ear position.

While dozing, watching a bird, or surveying its domain, a cat's ears are erect and facing forward; the pupils are usually constricted. In contrast, an aggressive cat that is on the offensive will rotate his still-erect ears until the backs of them face forward toward the recipient of the threat. Some investigators believe that how much of the backs is visible from the front indicates the severity of the threat. It may also be that he is carrying on auditory surveillance to avoid an unrelated attack from

DISPUTED TERRITORY
The social hierarchy is well understood by neighboring felids and minor squabbles over territory rarely result in serious wounds. In fights over more major issues, however, cats can end up in a sorry state.

behind while all his attention is focused on the threat he is facing.

Body posture of an aggressive cat includes standing with its back parallel to the ground or with its weight shifted forward to the front legs. The tail thrashes from side to side and low growling is audible.

Fighting When things get physical, it's usually two tomcats fighting over who is top cat or for the favors of a female in estrus. Fights occur mainly at night when toms are on the prowl and calling to females, who respond just as noisily.

Kittens fight with littermates as a way of learning the skills they will need as adults. While there is often a lot of mock aggression and growling, their teeth are so tiny that they do no real damage.

The cat hierarchy Top in the pecking order is the unneutered queen with the most kittens. Next come toms, with the best fighter

taking precedence. A contender must do battle and win to supplant a higher tom. Neutered males, with their lowered testosterone levels and lack of aggression, are always on the bottom level. The ranking is rigid and recognized by all the cats in a particular neighborhood.

PLAY FIGHTING
Kittens learn and practice the skills they need for hunting and self-defense during play sessions with siblings.

HUNTING

The cat has been described as the perfect killing machine. The method used is almost universal among cats great and small. Even though you may never see it in the wild, you can observe the very same hunting procedure being enacted in a suburban garden.

READY TO POUNCE
As he nears his prey, the hunter may make brief runs forward in a full crouch to maintain his low profile. When he is close enough, a burst of speed, a pounce and success or failure, depending on his skill.

The hunt begins with the cat cautiously stalking its prey. The instantly recognizable posture includes the cat's body crouching low with every muscle tense. The ears are flattened and drawn down to the side, and the eyes, seemingly unblinking, are riveted on the quarry.

With infinite patience, the cat moves closer and closer, freezing whenever the quarry shows any sign of alarm. The tail twitches in anticipation and the weight is transferred from haunch to haunch as the back feet take a firm foothold.

Although your pet cat is well fed, the instinct to hunt is very strong. He may present his victims to you as trophies, tokens of his affection, or simply to show you how smart he is.

It's only natural

It is something of a paradox that humans have always valued cats so greatly for their ability to reduce rodent numbers yet are so outraged when cats catch birds. We forget that the cat is only doing what comes naturally and cannot possibly understand the difference. Many owners are upset at what seems like cruelty in a cat's behavior, but when a cat plays with his victim, he is merely stunning it so that it can't escape. If it lies still, the cat rapidly loses interest.

If you are trying to rescue a bird or other inappropriate prey, try to distract your cat by creating some more interesting movement nearby in the bushes. Unfortunately, small birds often die of shock after such traumatic encounters. Some owners attach bells to their cat's collar to warn the birds, but these are not really very effective. It's probably best not to encourage birds into your garden, because your cat may find the temptation irresistible.

Suddenly, the cat makes a rush, covering the remaining distance at high speed. He pounces, grasping the victim with his paws and delivers a killing bite, forcing his long canine teeth between the bones of the neck. The spinal cord is stretched and torn.

With large cats and larger prey, the target area is sometimes the throat. The animal suffocates when the windpipe is squeezed or punctured.

WHAT'S THAT?
Your cat will check out anything unusual going on in his territory. Even when he seems to be drowsing in the sun, he will be instantly alert at any small movement.

COMMON BEHAVIORAL PROBLEMS

If you wish to train your cat not to do certain things, you must first try to understand *why* he does them. Some behavior problems can be dealt with quite simply, while others take a great deal of perseverance.

Scratching Because scratching is natural marking behavior, the best solution is to provide your cat with a scratching post. Encourage him to use it by rubbing dried catnip into it to make it smell inviting and placing it where he likes to scratch. Cover any furniture he's been using for the purpose with plastic or aluminum foil until he likes the post better.

Petting and biting Some cats that were not sufficiently socialized with humans as kittens develop a puzzling behavior. When they are

being petted, they suddenly switch from seeming to enjoy the handling to biting and scratching their owner's hand, sinking their teeth into the flesh with very real intent. Perhaps they suddenly feel trapped, so don't try to cuddle such a cat or hold it in your arms. Let the cat initiate the contact and let it feel free to come and go on your lap until it has enough confidence to want to stay.

Overgrooming When a cat is severely stressed, it may soothe itself by grooming over and over again to the point where it makes bare, sore patches on its legs, flanks, stomach and the base of the tail. Distract him with play and try to reduce his stress by making him feel more secure. If the behavior continues, you may have to ask your vet to prescribe a mild tranquilizer to help him cope with whatever is causing the stress.

Jealousy If you plan to introduce a new pet into your household, make sure your cat won't feel jealous. He could see the newcomer as a rival and treat it as an intruder, snarling and hissing and making it feel unwelcome. Most pets accept others eventually, but meanwhile, you must find ways to limit their contact with each other and give each one plenty of private time with you. Cage the newcomer and feed the animals together from separate bowls. With food to distract them they are less likely to show hostility. If your new pet is a kitten, it will become less annoying to your cat as it matures.

Stealing food The best way to prevent such behavior is not to leave food unattended. But realistically, there are always going to be times you forget. Try making a loud noise by hitting the table with a rolled-up newspaper when you catch him in the act. Or perhaps throw something soft or direct a squirt of water at him. Your cross voice and body language will deliver the message, but the temptation may be too strong.

SPRAYING AND SOILING

Although this is natural behavior, just a way of sending messages, spraying and soiling can cause problems for owners. Try to understand how he sees his world. In the long run, you and he may both have to make a few compromises.

STAKING HIS CLAIM
This ginger tomcat is leaving the scent of his skin secretions on this sunny wall to warn neighboring cats off. Cats have favored spots for various times of the day and regard takeover bids by other cats very seriously.

Territorial rights Cats are very conscious of their right to a certain territory and use four ways to send a "keep out" message to interlopers. Spraying urine at the boundaries sends an unmistakable signal to neighboring felines. Scratch marks do the same. The third way is to rub the side of the head against walls and corners to leave the scent of secretions from sebaceous glands in the skin. Leaving unburied feces is another token of their presence. The territory need not be large, but it must be clear that it is theirs.

Unfortunately, owners don't really appreciate the pungent stink of urine on potplants or around doorways. Even worse, some cats spray indoors, marking furniture and soft furnishings, especially in a multi-cat household. Both sexes spray but the urine of males, especially of tomcats, is more

WHO GOES THERE?
If your cat discovers that another cat has left a calling card on his territory, he will immediately cover it with his own scent.

offensive. The scent marks must be renewed constantly, because they relay all kinds of extra information to other cats, such as how recently the "owner" inspected his property.

Soiling can be an early sign that your cat is ill, or perhaps he is constipated and has abandoned his litter tray because he associates it with pain. Or maybe he simply

doesn't like the brand of litter you are buying.

Soiling can also indicate stress. Have you have had visitors, or tradesmen in the house doing renovations? Perhaps there is a new baby or a new pet?

If you can identify and remove the stress, do so. Otherwise clean the area thoroughly to get rid of the smell or he may repeat the act. Don't use pungent disinfectants with chlorine or ammonia, and always test your carpets and soft furnishings for color-fastness before using strong cleaning solutions.

Cats that are left alone for long periods may try a disconcerting way of reminding you that they're around. They may leave a small token on the middle of your bed. To discourage this unwelcome behavior,

SPRAYING
Standing stiffly, with tail erect, a cat will direct a small jet of urine over the object it wishes to mark. Some garden plants simply can't take it and eventually die.

throw a sheet of plastic over the bed to make it cold and uninviting.

Discouragement Once you have eliminated the smell, use sheets of plastic or aluminum foil to cover places your cat favors for soiling. Or, if possible, feed your cat in this place for a couple of weeks. No cat will soil close to where he eats.

ABOUT
BREEDING

Unless you are breeding purebred cats for a specific purpose, it is not recommended that you breed cats. You will simply be adding to the population of unwanted kittens and have the continual hassle of trying to find good homes for them. In fact, many shelters and cat protection organizations insist that all cats they sell are desexed. On the other hand, serious breeders find the challenge of producing particular characteristics in kittens addictive, and their enthusiasm survives late nights tending birthing queens, interrupted sleep, and constant expense. The rewards, however, have nothing to do with money, and everything to do with the cat's beauty and charm.

THE FEMALE CYCLE

The excitement of breeding a cat to meet its standard is addictive and can last for a lifetime. Be warned, though, that very few, if any, breeders actually make a profit.

INTERMISSION
After mating, the queen will roll about and clean herself. She will then, in a very short space of time, be ready to mate again and will start flirting with the tomcat.

When a female cat, or queen, is ready to mate, she is said to be in season, in estrus, or in heat. When she comes in season, she will emit loud cries, or calls, to attract a tomcat. She will also crouch down and creep about the floor on slightly bent legs, and may even spray.

As her season progresses she will rub against you or an article of furniture, raise her rear end into the air and make alluring little noises. You will also notice that her vulva is swollen and some clear discharge may be visible.

Frequency of seasons The outdoor queen will come in season in spring and again in early fall. If exposed to the right amount of artificial light, the indoor queen may cycle in and out of season every few weeks throughout the entire year until she is bred. Frequent seasons pose problems for your queen. She has a greater chance of contracting a uterine infection. If she has young kittens, another pregnancy will deplete her supplies of vitamins, minerals and calcium and really wear her down. Many females will not eat

when in season and can become dangerously thin.

If you don't want your queen to fall pregnant at a particular time, but want her to remain intact for future breeding, you must confine either her or the studcat.

The mating ritual When the female is fully in season and ready to accept the male, she will flirt with him, rub her cheek on the floor and then offer him her backside, holding her tail to one side. He will jump on her and grab the back of her neck with his teeth. This usually subdues her and she will submit. He then straddles her and proceeds to enter her from the rear. He breeds her quickly and, when penetration is achieved, she will let loose a blood-curdling shriek. The wise male will hurry to remove himself from her proximity before she turns and strikes out at him with her claws. She then rolls about on the floor for several minutes, making noises, after which she will sit up and clean herself thoroughly, preparing herself for a repeat performance.

Within about ten minutes, she is back at him again with her coy little noises, head rubbing and flirtatious ways. He will respond as before and the process is repeated.

Mating for pregnancy To achieve pregnancy, it is generally best to allow cats to mate several times over one or two days. Some males and females can be left together; others must be separated to avoid fights.

AVERAGE LITTER SIZE IS THREE OR FOUR KITTENS
There is no truth to the notion that breeding your queen either early or late in her season will result in her having fewer kittens. It is also untrue that you can dictate how many males and females she will have by breeding on a certain day of her season. The male determines the sex and the female determines the number in the litter.

CHOOSING A STUD

Before you consider breeding cats, ask yourself if you are willing to sit up all night with an expectant queen, or to give up your annual vacation because you cannot leave a house full of cats!

What to look for When selecting the ideal partner for your queen, ask to see his pedigree, or family tree. In addition to the colors of his ancestors listed on the chart, ask if his owner knows the colors of his litter mates. These cats do not appear on the pedigree but can indicate the colors of the kittens your female will produce. For instance, the pedigree might simply show seal points, but two seal points can produce a blue point if their ancestors' litter mates or their litter mates are blue points.

Many breeders choose a studcat based on the number of champions

THE STUD HIMSELF
The studcat's owner should provide you with a five-generation pedigree, but a minimum of three generations is acceptable if you do not plan to show.

and grand champions in his pedigree. For many reasons, cats may not have been shown, yet their bloodlines may be identical to others who have been shown. What's important is the bloodline, and you should look for the traits and health information carried in the bloodline.

Select a male to complement your female. If she has a long tail and her standard calls for a short tail, choose a male with a short tail. The queen will have some kittens with long tails and some with short tails.

Clean and healthy It is important to find a studcat who comes from healthy stock and is in good health. Make sure both your queen and the studcat have current vaccinations.

Your female must go to the studcat. He does not come to her. Visit the quarters where the studcat is housed. In many cases, this will be a large cage in someone's home or a cage in a shed or garage. Check that his bedding, litter pan, and general surroundings are clean. You can expect to find a strong odor in his quarters. The studcat's urine, both in his litter pan and where he has sprayed, is strong. This does not mean he is not clean—no amount of cleaning will take away that odor.

Make sure his quarters are free from drafts and climate-controlled. Check with his owner if she will be present during mating to ensure the stud doesn't hurt your queen, or vice versa. An ethical breeder will witness the matings and be able to tell you that mating definitely took place. With an unethical one you cannot be sure your queen has had a fair chance of becoming pregnant.

NO NASTY SURPRISES
Before sending your queen to the studcat for mating, settle the cost of the service and find out if a free repeat breeding will be offered in the event she either doesn't conceive or has only one kitten.

Settling in Even if your queen is in season and howling for a male, don't be surprised if she goes out of season with the stress of the journey to the studcat's home. The queen should not be put in with the male immediately, whether she is in or out of season. She should be placed in a cage next to his. She will usually relax and start to rub herself against the bars of the cage nearest his. That is when the breeder can place her in the cage with the male. If she does nothing but curl up and hiss and growl, you may be asked to take her home and try again another time.

If your queen goes out of season from the stress of the trip, the breeder may keep her for a few weeks until she can be bred.

PREGNANCY

Be aware of your queen's needs and try to make her pregnancy as easy as possible. Although her behavior may change significantly during this time, this is perfectly natural and not a cause for concern.

Morning sickness, one of the first signs that your queen is pregnant, appears during the first ten days of pregnancy. It generally lasts for only about 48 hours, during which time she will vomit several times a day. Take special care of her as she is at her most vulnerable and there is a high risk of miscarriage.

Avoid taking your pregnant queen anywhere during this time—even the germs at the vet's are a hazard. Handle her very gently, particularly during the first few weeks, and do not let anyone carry her roughly.

At about three weeks, turn her over on her back and look at her nipples. They should be turning pink and starting to enlarge. You will also notice at this point that she has become swollen around her vulva; this is more easily seen on shorthaired or light-colored queens.

Temperament changes

Your pregnant queen's temperament may change—for better or for worse. She is helpless in the face of the hormonal changes going on in her body and may not want other cats near her. She may even attack one of her favorite companions. This is natural behavior, so don't punish her. It may be best to confine her to a room or confine the other pets until this phase passes.

A DAILY CLEANSE

During the last few weeks of your queen's pregnancy, you may need to gently clean the area around her anus with a soft cloth and water. As with this Siamese, her increased girth sometimes makes it difficult for her to reach around to clean herself properly.

As she progresses through her pregnancy, her temperament will probably change yet again and she may actually seek out other cats. She'll want to cuddle up to them and will even allow them to nurse on her. She is in full maternal bloom. Don't be surprised if she picks up a soft toy in her mouth and carries it about the house, mewing softly. This is her make-believe kitten and she is practicing being a mother.

Appetite changes Although your queen is supposed to eat more while pregnant, some queens don't experience an increase in appetite. If she is otherwise in good health, do not worry. Just check with your vet about adding vitamins or calcium to her diet. It may be that her current diet is sufficient.

Keep a close eye Watch closely throughout your queen's pregnancy for any signs of illness or listlessness. If you spot these signs, take her to the vet as she could be suffering from a uterine infection or false pregnancy, or she could be having a miscarriage.

Make sure you record the exact date that she was bred as this is vital information for your vet in determining the possible causes of her problem. It is also important for you to know this in order to prepare for the birth and to be on hand when she delivers.

A cat will generally carry kittens for 63 days, although she can have them as early as 58 or 59 days and as late as 67 or 68 days with no ill effects. Any period of time shorter or longer than these generally indicates trouble, and you should seek the advice of your vet.

TEMPERAMENT CHANGES
During pregnancy, your queen, like this Siamese chocolate lynx point, may show you more affection, and expect more attention. She may fall asleep purring while you gently stroke her tummy.

Delivery room When your queen becomes pregnant, prepare a place for her to deliver her kittens. If she is a cattery cat, her cage will be fine, but if she is your house cat, a half-pulled-out drawer lined with soft cloth may be suitable. A box on the floor of a closet with the door ajar is also a good site. She may, however, prefer to choose the place herself.

BIRTHING

Watching your queen give birth is one of the most amazing and satisfying parts of breeding. Although she will generally need no assistance while giving birth, your queen will appreciate your presence, particularly if anything should go wrong.

When your queen is approaching her 59th day of pregnancy, you should confine her to the cage or room in which she is to deliver her kittens. She may fool you into thinking that birth is imminent by scratching and tearing at the paper or toweling in the birthing box, becoming very restless and not wanting much to eat. These signs can go on for one to two weeks and are not reliable indicators of labor. In some cases these signs may start when she is mated.

Her temperature will drop to below 101.2°F (38.4°C) for a 24-hour period before delivery, but don't take her temperature at this time, unless she is very used to it, as it could stress her. Other definitive signs are a tightening of the skin over her abdomen and the movement. She will meow quite plaintively during this time.

Labor Be alert to any signs that labor has begun. You will notice her squatting and straining and, if she is shorthaired, you may also see labor contractions rippling. If she is longhaired, you will have cut away the hair from around her vagina so the hair doesn't stick to the umbilical cord during delivery. You also should have trimmed the hair from around her nipples so the kittens can suck on them more easily. For shorthairs, these preparations are not necessary.

The birth You will usually see a greenish mucus discharge from the vaginal opening when birth is imminent. You should be on hand to comfort your queen but do not be too hasty about stepping in to help. You may do more harm than good.

The queen should deliver the first kitten within 15 minutes of her first beginning to crouch, strain and cry, and she will purr throughout the entire delivery. The remaining kittens will be delivered at intervals of between 5 and 30 minutes.

If the kitten is delivered head first, the queen should need no help. If it is delivered feet first (breech birth) and it does not arrive for five minutes or so, you will need to help. Make sure your hands are clean,

DELIVERING

The queen delivers her first kitten within about 15 minutes of the onset of labor. Depending on the number of kittens, labor will last for up to two or three hours.

CLEANING

After giving birth, the queen will chew off the umbilical cord and eat the placenta, which provides her with many nutrients. In the wild this is vital safeguard because the smell would attract predators. She will then clean her kittens.

NURSING

Soon after being born, the kittens will shakily make their way around to their mother's nipples and start feeding.

MOTHER CARE

The queen will feed and clean her kittens, and eat their urine and excrement to keep the nest clean until they are able to use a litter pan—usually at about three weeks of age.

BIRTHING continued

FEEDING TIME
The queen will nurse her kittens until they are about three weeks of age. At this time they will start eating semi-solid and solid foods.

wrap a soft towel around the kitten's body and gently manipulate him, trying to coordinate with the mother's contractions, if possible. Do not pull on the tail or the legs or they will come off in your hands. Do not squeeze the abdomen, either.

If labor continues and no kittens appear for more than an hour, or if a kitten or two have been born and labor goes on for another hour or so without another kitten appearing, call the vet. If you allow labor to go on too long, you risk not only having the kittens die but possibly losing your queen as well.

The first breath After giving birth, most queens will immediately open the sacs over the kittens' faces so that they can take their first breath. If this is your queen's first litter and she is struggling, or if she doesn't open the sacs straight away, you should tear them open with your nails. Then place each kitten near the queen's mouth so that she can stimulate breathing by licking them.

If any of the kittens appear to be in distress, dry them and keep them warm. Then you will just have to let nature take its course.

Most queens will chew off the umbilical cord and eat the placenta. Give her 15 minutes or so to do this. Then if she still hasn't cut the cord, you can do so by tying a piece of string around the umbilical cord about 1 inch (2.5 cm) from the kitten's stomach. Using sterilized scissors, cut the cord on the outside of the string, farthest from the kitten's stomach. Or, using your fingernails, clamp the cord tightly, and using a scissor motion, cut back and forth, until the cord is severed. Then, with the sterilized scissors, cut the cord, again about one inch (2.5 cm) from the kitten's abdomen.

The queen will generally eat the placenta and excess umbilical cord. She does this not only because they supply her with essential nutrients but also because of her instinctive fear that predators will be attracted by them. She will then wash her kittens, and at this stage you may want to weigh the newborns.

Post-birth Your vet may suggest that your queen have a shot of oxytocin within 12 hours of giving birth. In some countries this can be administered at home; in others you must take your queen to the vet. This shot is given to make sure that there are no remnants of placenta left in her uterus that might cause infection. It also helps to induce the milk supply. Your vet may also recommend that the queen be put on

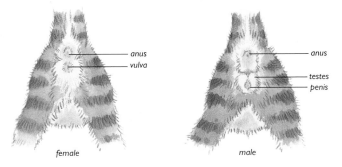

female

male

DETERMINING SEX
To determine the sex of a kitten, gently lift its tail and check against the drawings above. Note the greater distance between the anus and the urogenital orifice in the male.

an antibiotic for seven to ten days to ward off any minor infections the kittens might catch while nursing.

Provide your queen with clean bedding, and make sure she and the kittens are housed in a dimly lit place, away from drafts and the hustle and bustle of the household. The ideal room temperature is 70°F (21°C). If this is not possible and the

room is cold, an infrared heating light or a heating pad placed under the toweling is recommended. If, on the other hand, the room is too hot, the queen will separate herself from the kittens to cool them down.

Always place her food, water and litter pan within easy reach as the queen will not want to leave her kittens, even for a short time.

CARING FOR NEWBORNS

Trust your queen. She knows what's best for her kittens and she will wean them when she sees fit. When they start to sample adult food, at about three weeks, place a litter pan nearby. They will quickly learn to use it by watching their mother.

ORPHAN KITTENS

If the worst happens and your queen dies during delivery, or if she has a Cesarean section to aid in delivery, you may have to become the kittens' mother. Try feeding them with nursing bottles made especially for kittens (obtainable from your vet). Or use a syringe or an eye dropper.

When kittens are between seven and ten days old, their eyes should open. If they don't, blot them very gently with cotton balls dipped in warm water until they do. Very often, when the eyes open there will be a squirt of creamy-looking pus, which should be gently cleaned away. If not removed, it can lead to eye disorders, including scarring and blindness.

Check the eyes often, administer any eye ointment your vet has prescribed and repeat the bathing process regularly to ensure that the kittens' eyes remain open and clean. Aside from changing the queen's bedding, feeding her, and making sure the kittens' eyes are clean, there is very little to do for the next two or three weeks. It is a good idea to pick the kittens up every day, turn them over on their backs and stroke their stomachs. This accustoms them to being handled and also gives you an opportunity to check their health. By holding the kittens up to your face you can tell if they smell. The healthy kitten will have absolutely no odor, while the kitten with a health problem will.

Cleaning and feeding The mother will clean the kittens and consume their urine and excrement until the kittens start using the litter pan. This usually happens when they are introduced to semi-solid food at three to four weeks of age, although this will vary depending on the kittens' health and size and the mother's milk supply. Goat's milk, evaporated milk, baby cereal and egg yolk all make good starter foods.

Orphan kittens You must provide a source of heat, such as a heating pad or infrared lamp, and keep the kittens away from drafts. You can purchase kitten milk formulas from your vet or a pet store, but these do not contain all the nutrients and antibodies of their mother's milk. Give just a few drops of formula at room temperature each time as their stomachs are very small. For the first week, feed the kittens every two hours. After each feeding, take a soft cloth and gently wipe the genitals and rectum to stimulate them to excrete. Then wash their faces and bottoms with another cloth. As the kittens eat more, increase the time between feedings.

Developing kittens Once the kittens start walking around, initiate gentle play by trailing a ribbon for them to follow. Their eyes are not well focused at this age, and they're not coordinated, so don't expect too much of them. Don't place them on high surfaces until they are older and can recognize the dangers.

WARM AS TOAST
Kittens will keep warm by snuggling up together with the queen. In cooler climates, you may want to give them some extra warmth by providing them with a heated cat bed.

SHOWING YOUR CAT

While not every breeder participates in the fun and madness of showing their "wares", for many it's something they wouldn't miss for the world. Shows offer breeders and cat enthusiasts alike a chance to socialize and compare notes, and to see the most perfect examples of the various breeds, as well as many adored non-pedigreed cats. Cat shows are also a great place to visit if you want a cat but still can't decide which breed is for you. A word of warning, though: you are certain to fall in love with far more cats than you can possibly own in one lifetime, so don't get carried away.

ABOUT PEDIGREES AND GENETICS

As more and more information is gathered about genes and inherited traits, cat breeding is becoming quite a science, with almost unlimited possibilities. Guidelines for the various breeds are, however, strict, and only animals that conform can become champions.

Gene complement Every kitten inherits an equal number of genes from both parents but in a litter of, say, five, every kitten may be slightly or dramatically different because the genes are arranged in different orders along the bead-like chromosome chain. The chromosomes carry the genetic blueprint for the individual's total makeup.

Gene manipulation The main purpose behind a calculated breeding program is to produce offspring with certain characteristics, be it temperament, body shape, eye color or a new color combination to add to the countless colors already available. The breeder chooses breeding stock with the desired features and enhances the traits by breeding to individuals with similar or complementary desirable traits.

To be successful, breeders must have a good understanding of the information that lies hidden (to the novice) in the written pedigree that comes with every pure-bred cat.

To achieve particular color combinations, with or without shading or tipping, the breeder

LITTERMATES
Breeding for color, as for other traits, is a lottery, but a careful selection and mating program increases the odds for a successful outcome.

needs to understand how dominant and recessive genes operate, because some colors are recessive and two recessive genes cannot produce a dominant, so the desired color may be lost.

Linked genes Some inherited characteristics are linked to gender, which means they can appear only in kittens of a particular sex. Tortoiseshell cats, for example, are always female. Other links govern eye and coat color matches.

Dominant and recessive genes
In the struggle for supremacy within the fertilized egg, the trait on a dominant gene is most likely to appear in the kitten. For example, some eye colors are more likely to be passed on than others, and tabby colors will take precedence over solid colors. The majority of feral cats are tabby because over several generations in the wild the tabby gene overwhelms the rest.

Undesirable traits Some genes carry undesirable characteristics with them. For example, white cats with blue eyes are sometimes deaf and a white cat with odd eyes may be deaf on the side with the blue eye. Some Siamese cats carry a gene that causes them to squint to correct their double vision, and breeders are at pains to breed out this fault.

Mutations From time to time, mutations occur spontaneously and these can result in the development of a new breed. In such cases, acceptance by the Cat Fancy and the other official associations will be delayed until it is certain that breeding the mutant strain carries no risk of related genetic defects. A good example of a recent new breed is the American Wirehair (see p. 216), with her crimped, coiled, springy coat. In the Scottish Fold, the folded ears are the result of a cartilage abnormality. If two such cats are bred, the kittens will be crippled.

Red lynx point
Oriental Shorthair

PREPARING FOR THE SHOW

Although plenty of hard work goes into preparing your cat for the show ring, this should also be lots of fun. And the thrill of having her shown and win a ribbon makes it all worthwhile.

GETTING READY
Once you have been to a few shows, and learned many of the grooming tricks, you'll be able to present your cat as attractively as this seal point Birman.

To be shown, all cats must be healthy and free from ticks, lice, fleas, ringworm and any other parasites. If your cat has been in contact with a contagious disease within 21 days of the show, then she is not eligible to be shown. You must also ensure that she is current on her vaccinations, and it is sometimes helpful to give the show cat more frequent booster shots, but check this with your vet. Shows in the US no longer demand a veterinary inspection of your cat before she is admitted to the show hall. In other countries, each cat is first examined by a vet and certified free of disease and/or parasites.

Grooming for showing Your cat should be bathed before a show. Clip her nails prior to bathing, and be sure to clean her ears. A shorthaired cat needs only a quick brush and her coat slicked down with your hand or a chamois; a longhaired cat requires a lot more effort.

The longhaired cat cannot wait until show time for her bath. If she is being shown regularly, she must be bathed weekly and combed twice daily to avoid mats and tangles, lessen shedding and promote a healthier coat. You will also learn some grooming tricks over time. For example, to moderate the apparent

size of the ears, fluff up the hair on the top of her head. To make her tail appear shorter, tweak off the excess hair at the end of the tail. To make her neck look thicker and shorter, comb out her ruff so that it stands out to conceal her neck and frame her face. Some professionals cut the hair over the eyes to make the eyes look rounder, and clip the hair around the face to give it a rounded look. When preparing her for the show, consult with professionals.

Entering your cat There are different rules for showing a cat in every association in every country. But to be eligible for showing, most associations require that all cats over the age of eight months are registered. Generally, you must enter your cat at least four weeks ahead. Fill out an entry form obtained from the entry clerk and send it back with the fee. Some clubs accept entries up to the week before the show, but most shows limit entry numbers.

Classes In the US, the kitten class is for kittens four to eight months old. Over eight months of age, your cat will compete as an adult in the open class. If she takes a certain number of winner ribbons, or points, she gains the title Champion. After she has been shown as a Champion, she must again earn a certain number of points to become Grand Champion.

There are seven registries in North America with differing requirements for showing, so check with the one in your area. Some associations offer further titles of Master Grand Champion and Supreme Grand Champion. Household pets can also earn titles on a similar point system.

Shows offer classes for neutered or spayed cats. Adult neuters and spays are shown in the altered class, while neutered or spayed kittens four to eight months old are still shown in the kitten class. Altered class titles are Champion, Grand Champion and Master Grand Champion. There are no titles in the kitten classes.

AT THE SHOW

For aficionados, cat shows are lively and entertaining affairs, well worth the effort involved in preparing entrants. They are usually held in winter when the coats, especially of longhairs, are thick and luxuriant and seen at their very best.

THE FINISHING TOUCHES
Before taking your cat to the ring for judging, be sure to make the final touches to her coat to ensure that she is presented at her absolute best.

The show begins

When you arrive, you will be given a cage for your cat with an entry number attached, as well as a show catalog. The catalog lists the entrants' names and vital statistics as well as the classes in which the cats are entered. Be sure to check that all the information on your cat is accurate. If you should find an error, contact the show management immediately to have a correction made. Failure to do so may result in the voiding of wins or points your cat may earn. The catalog will also contain a schedule detailing the order in which the judging of the different classes will take place.

US shows In the US, judging is conducted in a manner far different from that of other countries. The owner carries her cat to the judging ring and places her in a judging cage. Chairs are provided in each ring so that you may sit and watch your cat being judged. Keep talking to a minimum because it can be distracting to a judge and too many loud voices can upset your cat, who may already be frightened by being handled by a stranger.

Some shows in the US will have between four and 12 judging rings at a time with each cat being judged separately by four to 12 judges. Each judge conducts "her own" show. The first judge takes the cat out of the cage, sets it on the judging table and examines it thoroughly. The judge will check for muscle tone, obesity, muscle development, coat texture, sex of the cat (if unaltered), eye shape, skull formation under the fur, ear set, boning in the legs, length of tail, shape of feet and soundness of the coat. She then returns the cat to the judging cage and washes her hands and the judging table with a disinfectant. She records any comments or awards to be given in the judging book, and hangs the appropriate ribbon, if any, on the cat's cage. Each cat is similarly judged by all the judges in the rings and they, in turn, hang the relevant ribbon, if any, on the cage.

Each cat competes within its own sex and color class and then competes for Best of Breed. Ultimately, each judge will select 10 cats (unaltered, altered or kittens) for her top ten Best-in-Show awards.

The numbers for the cats so chosen are placed on top of the judging cages and the owners place their cats in the appropriate cages. The judge normally takes each cat out of the cage and presents it to the audience, listing its attributes. She then returns it to the cage and hangs the corresponding ribbon on the cage, for example, Tenth Best Cat. This procedure is followed until the Best Cat is proudly displayed.

After your cat has been judged and, if successful, a ribbon hung on her cage, the ring clerk will let you know when to return her to her exhibition cage. Pay attention to the loud speaker as there is a chance that your cat will be called back for tie-breakers or even for a final award.

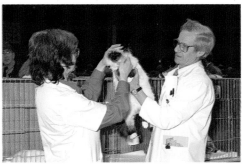

THE JUDGING
A steward holds a cat for the judge to examine.

What to take It's a good idea to take along: a small litter pan; water and food dishes; cat food; comb; brush; cotton swabs; powder (cornstarch, talcum powder or Fuller's earth); paper towels; cat toys; cage curtains (to cover back, two sides and top of cage); rug or towel for base of cage; bed; garbage bags (for litter); food and beverages (for you).

DIFFERENT NATIONAL STANDARDS

The notion of selective breeding and producing pedigreed cats has been around for less than two centuries and it has been largely the stimulus of showing cats that has lead to the spectrum of breeds and colors we have today.

The various associations, including The International Cat Association (TICA), the American Cat Association (ACA) and Cat Fanciers Association (CFA), are the main sponsors of cat shows, along with some breed associations and some large pet supplies companies. The aim is to present outstanding examples of the various breeds and to maintain competition among breeders in the quest for excellence.

International standards
Show requirements and breed specifications vary from country to

MORE THAN CUTE
These Persian blue kittens would be entered in one of several major categories for kittens up to eight months old.

country so to be absolutely certain your cat complies, get a copy of the Breed Standards used by the association holding the show you wish your cat to enter. Shows usually go on for a whole day, but some in the US may last for two days.

The judges bring considerable experience and expertise to their task and points are awarded according to how well your cat measures up against the standard for her breed (see Cat Breeds, starting on p. 202). There is a separate class for neutered or altered cats.

Judges In North America, the judge may broadcast a running commentary while she is judging, but in Britain and Europe, shows are run more conservatively.

A typical judging system

To give you some idea of the points taken into account during judging, here are TICA's levels of achievement among Championship and Household categories.

Champions (Pedigreed cats):
Kitten; Novice; Champion; Grand Champion; Double Grand Champion; Triple Grand Champion; Quadruple Grand Champion; Supreme Champion.

Household:
Kitten; Senior; Master; Grand Master; Double Grand Master; Triple Grand Master; Quadruple Grand Master; Supreme Grand Master.
.. Judges award 100 points, based on the breed's characteristics for head, ears, eyes, body, bone structure and tail. These points are distributed differently for each of the breeds (see TICA Standards, obtainable for the association).

There are various classes and divisions. The judge selects the three best cats in each division; the best wins 25 points, the second 20 points and the third 15 points.

From among these winners, the judge selects the first, second and third Best of Breed No points are awarded for these selections, but these cats represent the "ideal" of their breed.

Rosettes are then awarded to the judge's choice of the Top Ten Cats within each major category. These cats are chosen primarily from the Best of Breed winners, although judges may select any cat they have judged during the show, provided it does not defeat a cat that has defeated it at a lower level.

Reaching a finals level means that the cat is considered to be among the very best in the show. The final awards carry points that are accumulated to attain championship rankings.

The major categories of championship cats and how they may enter: Kitten; Championship Adults; Alters; Household Pet Kittens; Household Pet Adults.

PART THREE

CAT BREEDS

How to Use This Guide

This guide provides details of 38 of the most popular breeds to help you find a cat that is just right for you.

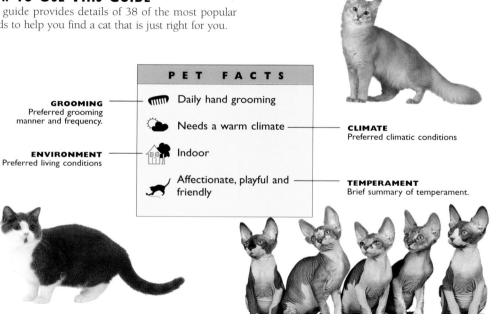

PET FACTS

GROOMING
Preferred grooming manner and frequency.

Daily hand grooming

Needs a warm climate

CLIMATE
Preferred climatic conditions

ENVIRONMENT
Preferred living conditions

Indoor

Affectionate, playful and friendly

TEMPERAMENT
Brief summary of temperament.

NAME OF BREED
These are presented alphabetically in shorthair and then longhair breeds.

INTRODUCTION
A brief overview of the breed and its characteristics.

PET FACTS
Daily hand grooming
Needs a warm climate
Indoor
Affectionate, playful and friendly

CORNISH REX
Playful and affectionate, the Cornish Rex is distinguished by its unusual wavy coat like that of the Rex rabbit, from which it derives its name. A born acrobat, lively and intelligent, it makes a fascinating pet.

blue mackerel tabby

OTHER IMAGES
A number of varieties of the breed are illustrated in different poses so the reader can easily identify the cat.

History These highly unusual cats originated quite spontaneously, probably from a mutated gene, in Cornwall, England, as the name indicates. The first Cornish Rex appeared in a litter born in 1950 and the breed has fascinated geneticists ever since. Although several individuals sent to the US in the late 1950s were developed independently of the Cornish strain, there is no noticeable difference between the two and, in fact, the Cornish strain is still predominant in the US today. It was first accepted for championship competition in the US in 1979 and is now accepted for competition worldwide.

calico

Description Lean and lithe bodied, the Cornish Rex has an arched back and a tucked-up stomach, something along the lines of a whippet. Its head is oval and comparatively small and its large ears are set high on the head. The high cheekbones and high-bridged Roman nose are unmistakable distinguidhing marks of the breed.

The medium-sized oval eyes are very wide set, but their color is of secondary importance and need not conform to the shade of the coat. Whatever the eye color, it should be clear and intense.

MAIN TEXT
Provides a detailed description of the breed, including its history, a description of its colors and coat patterns, and other distinguishing characteristics, as well as its temperament. There are also details of the grooming and climate requirements of the breed, and whether it is best suited to an indoor or outdoor life.

232

MAIN IMAGE
A good representative of the breed.

SHORTHAIRED CATS

As a result of cross-breeding, there is now a huge variety of hair lengths and types, from the Sphynx, with almost no hair, to the full, thick and flowing coat of the Persian. Between these two extremes are the shorthaired and medium-haired breeds. Some cats have double coats, while others are fine, silky and close lying. There are hundreds of color combinations. The hair on some cats is actually one of their more distinguishing features, for example, the Devon Rex, with its loose, soft waves, and the Cornish Rex, with its short, tight waves. With the shorthaired breeds, the elegance and lines of the body are easier to appreciate than in their less compact cousins, the longhairs.

PET FACTS

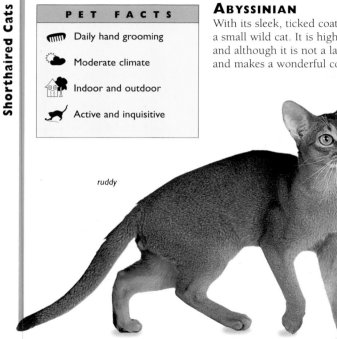

- Daily hand grooming
- Moderate climate
- Indoor and outdoor
- Active and inquisitive

ruddy

ABYSSINIAN

With its sleek, ticked coat, the Abyssinian strongly resembles a small wild cat. It is highly intelligent and extremely active, and although it is not a lap cat, it is loyal and affectionate and makes a wonderful companion.

History One of the world's oldest known breeds, the Abyssinian looks like the paintings and sculptures of ancient Egyptian cats and still retains the jungle look of *Felis lybica,* the African wildcat ancestor of all domestic cats.

Although its origin is uncertain, the early specimens of the breed were taken to Britain by soldiers returning from the Abyssinian War in 1868. The earliest Abyssinian taken to Britain was called Zula. Its owner was the wife of Captain Barrett-Lennard and its picture appeared in a book published in 1874. Zula bears little resemblance to today's Abyssinians.

The breed was first recognized as being separate in Britain in 1882 and although they were first exhibited in the US in 1909 they were not recognized as a separate breed there until 1986. Several top-quality Abyssinians that arrived in North America from England in the late 1930s form the foundation of today's American breeding programs.

Description The ideal Abyssinian has a slim body of medium size and length. Adult animals are lithe, hard and muscular with all physical elements of the cat in proportion. The head is a modified wedge and the brow, cheek and profile show a gentle contour with a slight nose break; the ears are large and alert. The almond-shaped eyes are large, brilliant and expressive and may be gold, green or hazel with a dark rim.

Abyssinians move gracefully on their fine-boned legs and give the

red

impression that they are standing on tiptoe. The tail is of medium length, broad at the base and tapered, without kinks.

The lustrous coat is beautiful to feel—soft, silky and fine in texture but also dense and resilient. The hair of this colorful cat should be long enough to accommodate dark, distinct bands of ticking.

Varieties In the United States, the Abyssinian comes in ruddy, red, blue and fawn. All colors must have at least two bands, preferably three, of ticking on each hair. Faint broken necklace marks around the throat are faults, and a solid unbroken necklace is cause for disqualification on the show bench.

The ruddy Abyssinian is a burnt sienna color, ticked with black or

blue

dark brown. The undercoat and inside of the forelegs and belly are a paler orange-brown and should be free of tabby markings. The ears and tail are tipped with black or dark brown, the paw pads are dark brown and the nose leather is tile red.

The red, or sorrel, Abyssinian is a warm, rich red, distinctly ticked with reddish brown. Deeper shades of red are preferred with an undercoat of apricot. The ears and tail are tipped with reddish brown and the paw pads and nose leather are rosy pink.

The blue Abyssinian is a soft, warm blue, ticked with various shades of slate blue. The undercoat and inside of the forelegs and belly are a warm cream to beige. The tail tip and outer tip of each hair is dark steel blue. The paw pads are mauve and the nose leather is dark pink.

The fawn Abyssinian is a warm beige ticked with dusky fawn, the outer tips of the hairs being darkest. The undercoat and inside of the forelegs and belly should be an unmarked pale fawn. The ears and tail are tipped with dusky fawn or lilac, the paw pads are mauve and the nose leather is pink.

In addition to these four colors, The International Cat Association (TICA) also recognizes the Abyssinian in the following colors: sorrel silver, blue silver and fawn silver.

The sorrel silver Abyssinian is medium white to light sorrel, ticked with chocolate brown.

The blue silver Abyssinian is silvery blue-gray, ticked with a deeper blue. The underside color is white to pale cream.

The fawn silver Abyssinian has a silvery, pinkish buff body, ticked with a deeper shade of pinkish buff. The underside is white to pale oatmeal.

Temperament Highly intelligent, the gentle Abyssinian has a well-balanced temperament, is eager, active and shows a lively interest in

fawn

its surroundings. It is a great companion cat, delighting in your company and always curious to know what you are doing. However, don't expect it to settle down as a lap cat as it usually has far too much

unexpended energy. Confident, well-mannered and responsive, it loves to play and will quickly devise spontaneous little games to hold your attention. It has a small and bell-like voice.

white

PET FACTS

🐾 Regular combing

☁️ Can tolerate cold weather

🏠 Indoor and outdoor

🐈 Friendly, intelligent and independent

AMERICAN SHORTHAIR

A handsome and gentle companion, the hardy American Shorthair has earned its place on the hearth of American homes since pioneering days. Long-lived and problem-free, it gets along well with other family members, including dogs.

History The ancestors of today's American Shorthairs arrived in North America with the early European pioneers. They made themselves useful aboard ships by catching the rats that ate the food supplies and that spread disease among humans. Once ashore, these hard-working cats bred freely and eventually established themselves as North America's own shorthaired cat. Through the years they have been called both Domestic Shorthair and American Shorthair, but since the 1950s the latter term has prevailed. The first shorthair placed in the official US register in 1901 was an imported male British Shorthair

orange tabby. There is a large genetic component from the British Shorthair breed in the American Shorthair, however, these cats are now rather larger than their British cousin, with less rounded faces and longer legs and tails.

Description The medium to large American Shorthair is a true working cat. Its body should be strong, athletic and well proportioned. These cats are not fully grown until three or four years of age, with males usually being significantly larger than females. The head is large with a full-cheeked face, slightly longer than it is wide. The medium-length nose

silver classic tabby kittens

has a gentle concave rise in profile. The nose leather is in harmony with the coat color. The strong-jawed muzzle is squared, and mature males have definite jowls. The bright, clear eyes are large and wide with the upper lid shaped like half an almond and the lower lid a fully rounded curve. They should slant slightly up at the outside end and the color must conform to the coat color. The medium-sized ears are set fairly well apart and the expression

is both trusting and friendly.

The medium-length legs are sturdy and well muscled, and the paws are full and rounded with the pad color in harmony with the coat color. The medium-length tail tapers to a blunt tip and should have no kinks.

Short, thick, even and coarse in texture, the coat is dense enough to protect the cat from cold, moisture and superficial skin injuries. It thickens up considerably in winter, but is not as plush as that of the British Shorthair. Grooming entails no more than regular combing to remove dead hair and a wipe over with a damp chamois to make the coat shine.

Varieties There are more than 100 colors and patterns to choose from in the American Shorthair and everyone seems to have a favorite. This is just a tiny sampling.

Silver tabby: white ground color with dense black tabby markings

arranged in a specific pattern. The classic pattern is most distinctive and consists of one or more unbroken necklaces on the chest, three wide

blue classic tabby

213

chocolate chinchilla

circular lines forming a bullseye on either side of the body, ring marks on the tail, bracelet marks on the legs and a shape like a butterfly with outspread wings on the shoulders. It is sometimes referred to as the "jewelry" pattern. With its emerald eyes, the silver tabby is truly a show-stopper.

White: a pure glistening white fur. The nose leather and paw pads are pink and the eyes are brilliant copper, vivid blue or odd-eyed (one copper and one blue).

Black smoke: the undercoat is white with the end of each hair deeply tipped with black (until it moves, the cat looks solid black). The points and mask are black with only a narrow band of white on each hair near the skin. The nose leather and paw pads are black and the eyes are copper.

cream mackerel tabby

brown patched tabby

Blue tabby: the ground color, including lips and chin, is pale bluish ivory; the markings are deep blue. The nose leather is deep rose, the paw pads are rose and the eyes are brilliant copper.

Blue-cream: blue with clearly defined patches of solid cream well broken up all over the body, legs and tail. The nose leather and paw pads are blue and/or pink and the eyes are brilliant copper.

Shaded silver: white undercoat with black tipping shading down from the face, flanks and tail, from dark on the spine to white on the chin and the underparts of the body and tail; the legs should be the same shade as the face (the cat should look darker than a chinchilla). The rims of the eyes, lips and nose should be outlined in black. The nose leather is brick red, the paw pads are black and the eyes are blue or blue-green.

blue cream

Brown tabby: the ground color is coppery brown with dense black markings in any of the tabby patterns. The lips, chin and rings around the eyes are paler and the backs of the legs are black from the paw to the heel. The nose leather is brick red, the paw pads are black or brown and the eyes should be a brilliant copper.

Van bicolor: the body is mainly white with unbrindled patches of any one color, largely confined to the head. The nose leather and paw pads are pink or harmonize with the color of the patches, and the eyes are copper.

Blue: light blue (lighter shades preferred) and an even tone from the nose to the tip of the tail. A sound darker shade is more acceptable than a slightly patterned lighter shade. The nose leather and paw pads are blue and the eyes are copper.

Temperament No matter what the color and pattern combination, the American Shorthair displays the same even temperament and friendliness. It is a perfect companion, both indoors or to accompany you on outdoor treks. Its robust, muscular build and protective coat lend themselves to walks in the rain or in cold temperatures. The American Shorthair is an excellent hunter with quiet ways, combined with a gentle, playful nature, which makes it an ideal choice for families.

shaded silver

PET FACTS

- Occasional light brushing
- Can tolerate cool weather
- Indoor and outdoor
- Friendly to people and other animals

AMERICAN WIREHAIR

An attention-grabbing animal, with its extraordinary coarse, wiry coat, the American Wirehair is still quite a rare breed. It makes an intelligent and most affectionate pet, with a vast range of pattern and color possibilities, but for showing, it is the wiriness of the coat that is all-important.

History Every American Wirehair now traces its parentage back to Adam, the first known American Wirehair. He was one of a litter of six barn cats born in 1966 in Verona, New York. He had sparse, wiry hair, and every hair was crimped, coiled and springy, even the whiskers. Wirehaired cats had been observed in natural colonies from time to time in the past, but had died out with natural selection. Largely unknown outside North America, the breed was accepted for championship competition by the Cat Fanciers' Association of the US in 1978.

Description If you stroke the coat of an American Wirehair in one direction, it feels as soft as silk. But stroke it in the opposite direction, and it feels like a mass of steel wool.

A well-boned, medium to large cat with well-developed muscles, the Wirehair is very similar in type to the American Shorthair. The rounded head has prominent cheekbones and a well-developed muzzle and chin. The medium-sized ears are set wide apart on the head. In profile, the nose shows a gentle concave curve and the nose leather should harmonize with the coat color. The large, round eyes are bright and clear, not necessarily corresponding in color to coat color.

black and white bicolor

216

Sturdy legs, in proportion to the body, finish in compact paws with pad color in keeping with the coat. The tapered tail is medium length with a rounded tip.

Wirehair kittens are born with tightly curled coats. In the mature animal, the hard, frizzy, medium-length coat still feels springy, tight and resilient. Individual hairs, including the hairs inside the ears, are crimped, hooked or bent. The overall appearance of

brown mackerel tabby

wiriness and the coarseness and resilience of the coat is more important than the crimping of each hair. The density of the wired coat leads to ringlet formation rather than clean waves. Curly whiskers are also desirable. Grooming is minimal. An occasional brushing with a soft brush to remove dead hair is all that is required.

Varieties The Wirehair comes in any and all coat colors and patterns, except colorpoint, solid chocolate or solid lavender because these are evidence of hybridization with a Siamese or Himalayan. The wiriness of the coat is the only requirement for show purposes. Unfortunately, many of the kittens do not have the prized feature. Anyone breeding Wirehairs must be prepared to find good homes for such straight-coated cats not eligible for showing.

calico van

Temperament The American Wirehair is closely related to the American Shorthair, so you can expect it to have the same affable nature. The Wirehair is friendly and and adaptable and plays in a gentle manner, getting along famously with children and with other pets, including dogs. It is quiet and reserved with lovable ways.

BENGAL

With the striking rosettes of its wild forebear, the Asian Leopard Cat, on its coat, the Bengal looks like a small leopard. It can be spirited and requires careful handling.

black spotted leopard kittens

black spotted leopard

History   The present-day Bengal was created in the late 1970s by a Californian breeder who wanted to reproduce the spotted pattern, colors and facial qualities of the Asian Leopard Cat.

The only association that accepts the Bengal for championship showing in the United States is The International Cat Association (TICA). None of the other associations will allow it to enter, because their bylaws prohibit the showing of any cats with wild blood, no matter how far back in the pedigree it may be. The Bengal now holds championship status with TICA.

Description   Looking basically wild, the Bengal will wade through water with no hesitation. It is large, strong-boned and very muscular, particularly the male. The head is a broad modified wedge, longer than it is wide, with rounded contours, much like its wild ancestors, but slightly smaller in proportion to its body. The neck is thick-set, muscular and large in proportion to the head. The nose is large and wide with slightly puffed, brick red nose leather outlined in black. The muzzle is full and broad with large, prominent whisker pads. The large eyes are almond shaped. They are blue-green in the seal sepia tabby, seal mink tabby and brown tabby, and blue in the seal lynx point. The ears are short, similar to those of its wild ancestors.

The medium-length legs have large bones and the feet are large and round with black paw pads. The medium-length tail is thick, with a rounded black tip. The soft, thick, medium-length coat needs only occasional combing.

Varieties Ground colors of the Bengal may be ivory, cream, yellow, buff, light or dark tan, golden, orange and mahogany. It comes in both spotted and marbled patterns, which may be black, dark brown, brown, tan,

chocolate or bitter chocolate and cinnamon, and in brown tabby, seal lynx point, seal sepia tabby and seal mink tabby. The cheeks, chin and throat are white.

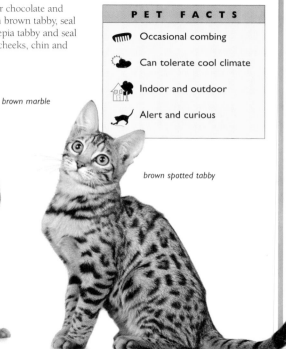

brown marble

brown spotted tabby

PET FACTS

- Occasional combing
- Can tolerate cool climate
- Indoor and outdoor
- Alert and curious

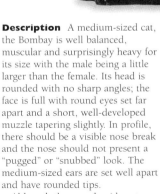

PET FACTS

- Daily hand grooming
- Warm climate
- Indoor
- Active, friendly and responsive

BOMBAY

The sleek and handsome Bombay cat has a gentle, loving nature and, although less vocal than many other breeds, rarely stops purring. It was named after India's black leopard, but the resemblance starts and ends with the sleek, gleaming coat.

kittens

History The result of crosses between the Burmese and black American Shorthairs, the Bombay was created in the late 1950s and early 1960s. Kentucky breeder Nikki Shuttleworth Horner, a keen fancier of the cross, was instrumental in having the new breed recognized and, after a lot of lobbying, championship status was awarded to the Bombay by the CFA in 1976. Other North American registries followed. The breed is rare outside the US and is still awaiting recognition in other countries, including Britain.

Description A medium-sized cat, the Bombay is well balanced, muscular and surprisingly heavy for its size with the male being a little larger than the female. Its head is rounded with no sharp angles; the face is full with round eyes set far apart and a short, well-developed muzzle tapering slightly. In profile, there should be a visible nose break and the nose should not present a "pugged" or "snubbed" look. The medium-sized ears are set well apart and have rounded tips.

Although the round, wide-set eyes may range in color from gold to a

deep, brilliant copper, deep-colored or copper eyes are considered superior by most fanciers.

The legs are medium length and in proportion to the body, and the feet are small and oval. The tail is medium length, straight and free of kinks. The nose leather and paw pads are black.

The coat should be very short, fine and close-lying, and should gleam like satin. The Bombay is a good example of a self-, or solid-colored cat, which means that the hair is one color from root to tip. The coat is extremely easy to groom, needing only regular combing with a fine-toothed comb to remove dead hair and perhaps a wipe over with a silk cloth or damp chamois to give it the shine of patent leather. Because little hair is shed, these cats are especially suited to a totally indoor situation.

Varieties The coat and color are considered so exceptional that in the standards of some American associations, half of the points (50) are allotted to the quality of the coat. The Bombay comes in only one color—black. Each hair must be jet black right down to the roots. In judging two Bombays with coats of equal merit, the depth of eye color would probably be a deciding factor in choosing the winner. Bombay kittens may start out with a rusty brown coat, but this matures to pure black.

Temperament Extremely smart and agile, Bombays love plenty of company, enjoy games and fetch naturally, but may become depressed or naughty if left home alone too much. Because they show great affection and their constant purring is so appealing, they make most satisfying pets. They are also assertive, hardy and healthy.

221

BRITISH SHORTHAIR

A robust and powerful cat with a rich, short, easy-care coat and a calm nature, the British Shorthair is a favorite in Britain, where it originated, and throughout the world. Its genes have contributed good qualities to many other breeds.

blue and white bicolor

red mackerel tabby

History Perhaps the oldest of the English breeds and one of the least altered, the British Shorthair traces its ancestry from the domestic cat of Rome, which became established in Britain during the time of the Roman Empire. This breed was first prized for its physical strength and hunting ability, but soon became equally valued for its gentle nature, endurance and loyalty. It is still a robust and healthy breed with none of the problems that some of the greatly modified breeds encounter. Because the original color was blue, the British Shorthair was at one time known as the British Blue. When

other colors, such as cream and then blue cream appeared, the name was simply changed to British Shorthair.

Although it was one of the first breeds to be shown in Britain late in the last century, it remained comparatively rare in the US until about 1964, when it was recognized for championship competition there. A similar European breed, derived from Chartreux and British Shorthairs, is called the European Shorthair, but it is judged to the British Shorthair standard.

There are two very distinct head types in the European Shorthair breed, according to whether Chartreux or British Shorthair predominates in the pedigree, and this makes judging difficult.

Description The British Shorthair is a medium to large cat with a compact, well-developed body and a full, broad chest. Its broad, round, massive head is set on a short, thick neck. The face and underlying bone structure are also rounded, as is the forehead, which is slightly flat on top of the head and should not slope. The medium-sized nose is broad and straight with the nose leather in keeping with the coat color. The chin is firm and in line with the nose and upper lip, and the muzzle is well developed with a definite stop behind large, round whisker pads. The large, round eyes are level and wide set, and come in copper. The medium-sized ears are broad at the base, with rounded tips.

The strong legs are short, well proportioned and heavily boned, with large, firm, round paws and paw pads that harmonize with the coat color. The tail is medium and thick and tapers to a rounded tip. The short, thick, single coat is dense and resilient. A weekly combing to remove dead hair is all that is needed to keep it looking good, although many owners have a repertoire of tricks to enhance the appearance for show purposes.

Varieties The British Shorthair comes in all colors and patterns, except solid chocolate, solid lilac and colorpoint. The tabby pattern is commonly seen in all colors in the classic, mackerel, ticked or spotted tabby form. The classic tabby pattern is discussed in the American Shorthair entry (see p. 212–215). Mackerel tabbies have narrow penciling of a darker shade all over the body, with rings on the chest and tail and even bars on the legs. In the

PET FACTS

- Weekly combing
- Can tolerate cooler weather
- Indoor and outdoor
- Playful and companionable, but rather reserved

blue

223

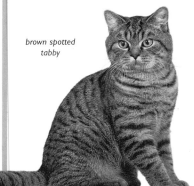

*brown spotted
tabby*

ticked tabby, each hair is ticked with bands of the shades of the ground and contrast colors, and the cat must have at least one distinct dark necklace. The spotted tabby has spots instead of stripes or pencil markings. The spots should not run together, except for a dorsal stripe running the length of the body and tail. The tail and legs are barred.

Some of the popular color and pattern combinations for the British Shorthair include:

Blue: light blue (lighter shades preferred) and an even tone from the nose to the tip of the tail. The nose leather and paw pads are blue and the eyes are copper.

Blue cream: the two colors cover the entire body in softly mingled patches (a blaze is desirable down the nose and under the chin, and a solid color on the legs, face or feet is a fault). The nose leather and paw pads are blue or pink, or mixed blue and pink and the eyes are copper. The blue cream combination occurs only on females, and blue cream kittens may look like plain blues at first.

Blue and white bicolor: mainly white with a certain percentage of distinct, unbrindled patches of blue distributed all over the body; a white blaze on the face is desirable. The nose leather and paw pads are blue or pink; the eyes are brilliant copper.

Red mackerel tabby: the ground color is rich red with the lips, chin and sides of feet darker; the mackerel pattern is a rich, vibrant, mahogany red. The forehead is marked with a characteristic "M" or "frown lines." The nose leather is brick red, the paw pads are deep red and the eyes are copper.

Blue spotted tabby: the ground color, including lips and chin, is pale bluish ivory with fawn overtones; spotted tabby markings are deep blue and the forehead is marked with a characteristic "M" or "frown lines." The nose leather and paw pads are blue or pink and the eyes are copper.

Cream spotted tabby: the ground color, including lips and chin, is pale cream; the spotted tabby markings are darker cream, but not too dark; the forehead is marked with a characteristic "M" or "frown lines." The nose leather and paw pads are pink and the eyes are copper.

Brown spotted tabby: the ground color, including lips and chin, is rich coppery brown; the spotted tabby markings are dense black; the forehead is marked with a characteristic "M" or "frown lines." The hind legs are black from the paw to the heel. The nose leather is brick red, the paw pads are black and the eyes are copper.

Black: glossy jet black with each hair an even tone from the root to the tip (no white hairs). The nose leather and paw pads are black and the eyes are brilliant copper.

Tortoiseshell and white (calico): bold patches of black and red on a white body (the three colors should be in roughly equal amounts; a blaze is desirable down the nose and under the chin). The nose leather is black or red, the paw pads are blue or pink, or a combination of the two, and the eyes are brilliant copper. The tortoiseshell and white combination occurs only on females.

Temperament The British Shorthair has a calm, gentle nature and is a loyal pet. Although it can be aloof, it becomes devoted to its owners, and makes a wonderful, undemanding companion that fits in well with family life. The female is an excellent mother.

cream spotted tabby

black

blue cream

225

platinum

PET FACTS

 Weekly combing

Needs warm climate

Indoor only

Affectionate, amusing and companionable

BURMESE

A sleek and elegant shorthair, the Burmese is agile and graceful with a delightful personality, good looks and great charm. Easy to look after, playful and tolerant of children, this is, many say, the perfect cat. Having lost many of the skills it needs to survive in the wild and being far too friendly and trusting for its own good, it should always be kept safe indoors.

History Although Burmese cats have been recorded in their country of origin for at least 500 years, the modern breed has been developed in the US only since 1930. The foundation animals were an Oriental-type female called Wong Mau, imported from Burma, and a seal point Siamese. At that time, the Siamese very much resembled the traditional Burmese in head and body characteristics. Probably no breed has endured quite as much controversy as the Burmese. The Cat Fanciers' Association (CFA) withdrew recognition of it in 1941 because there were too few cats with three generations of descendants that bred true to type, and the breed was not reinstated until 1956.

Although the original Burmese was a sable brown color, the only known brown cat in the fancy at that time, breeders began to produce other colors, notably champagne, in the early 1960s. The new colors caused an uproar, and the CFA opted to call them Malayan rather than Burmese, to soothe the ruffled feathers of those purists who bred only sable-colored Burmese.

blue

champagne

the new appearance, which is now called "Contemporary."

British breeders imported their first Burmese from the US in 1947 and the breed gained official recognition there in 1952. A whole spectrum of new colors and a lighter, more streamlined body, closer in type to the breed's Siamese ancestor has resulted from British breeding lines.

Description The US Burmese (pictured) is an altogether rounder and stockier animal than its counterparts in other countries. It has a

In the mid 1970s, a more serious controversy arose. A Burmese with facial features markedly different from the standard and from other Burmese was exhibited. The nose was so much shorter and the muzzle so much broader that it looked more like a brown Exotic Shorthair. Predictably, some judges pounced on this exhibit, pronounced it of "extreme type," and awarded it points over other Burmese. Naturally, many breeders rushed to purchase this "extreme type" Burmese, but

defects soon began to appear in kittens to such an extent that few survived, and those that did had to have surgery to correct eye defects and cleft palates. The problem became so serious that in 1979 Cornell University set up a five-year study that revealed that the "extreme type" carried certain genetic flaws. The country remains divided with some preferring to retain the look and stamina of the traditional Burmese and others breeding to achieve

blue

227

compact, dense, medium-sized body with substantial bone structure and good muscle development. Its chest is rounded and the back is straight from the shoulders to the hips, with the hips as wide as the chest.

The head is a rounded, medium-sized wedge, with a full face and considerable breadth between the eyes. A broad, short, well-developed muzzle maintains the rounded

sable

contours of the head. In profile, there is a visible nose break and the chin is firmly rounded.

The nose leather should harmonize with the coat color. The medium-length neck is well developed. The large, shining, expressive eyes are well rounded, set far apart and are a deep gold color. The medium-sized ears are set well apart and have rounded tips.

The legs are medium length and are well proportioned with small, round paws in the US (oval paws in Britain) and the color of the paw pads will be in keeping with the coat color. The tapered, medium-length tail should be straight with no kinks.

The gleaming coat is short, fine and satiny, and lies close to the body. Grooming entails only a weekly combing to remove dead hair and a wipe over with a damp chamois to enhance the natural shine.

sable

Varieties In the US, Burmese come in only four colors—sable, champagne, blue and platinum. In other countries, they also come in brown, blue, chocolate, lilac, red, cream, brown tortie, blue tortie, chocolate tortie and lilac tortie.

Sable (also known as brown) is the original and perhaps most striking color: the hair is rich, warm, sable brown, right down to the roots, shading to a lighter tone on the underparts. The nose leather and paw pads are brown and the eyes are brilliant yellow to gold.

Champagne (also known as chocolate): the hair is rich, warm, honey beige, with slightly darker shadings on the face and ears allowed. The nose

champagne

leather is light warm brown, the paw pads are pinkish-tan and the eyes are brilliant, deep golden yellow.

Blue: the hair is rich blue, right down to the roots, shading to a lighter tone on the underparts. The nose leather and paw pads are slate gray with a pinkish tinge and the eyes are brilliant golden yellow. The ears, face and feet all have a silvery shine.

Platinum (also known as lilac): the hair is pale, soft, silvery gray; ears and mask are slightly darker. The nose leather and paw pads are lavender-pink and the eyes are brilliant, deep golden yellow.

Temperament Burmese are extremely friendly to both strangers and family and communicate in sweet, soft voices. They crave attention and affection and will do anything to get it. They remain playful well into adulthood and dislike being left alone for long periods. If yours is a household

where humans are absent throughout the day, perhaps you should consider keeping two cats for company. Females assume an active role in running the house, while males are more laid back and prefer to supervise from someone's lap.

platinum

CHARTREUX

The sturdy French Chartreux is much admired for its hunting prowess and its dense, water-resistant fur. Its beautiful thick blue-gray coat has silver highlights and is set off by brilliant orange eyes.

kittens

History Noted in French documents as early as the sixteenth century, the first Chartreux cats are thought to have been kept by Carthusian monks at the Grenoble monastery where the famous Chartreuse liqueur was made. The cats probably earned their keep by keeping rat and mice numbers down, and this home may be the origin of the breed's name, although there are many other possibilities. The Chartreux was first exhibited in Paris in 1931 by one of the Leger sisters, keen breeders from Brittany. Three of the first ten Chartreux to go to the US in 1970 were obtained from the Legers' stock. In the US, the breed is classed as completely separate from the very similar blue British Shorthair, and received championship status in 1983.

Description The chunky body of the Chartreux is medium length and solidly muscled, with broad shoulders and a deep chest, males being larger and heavier than females. Boning is strong and muscle mass is dense.

The head is rounded and broad with powerful jaws, full cheeks and a softly contoured forehead. The nose is straight, medium length and width, with a slight stop at eye level.

The muzzle is comparatively small, narrow and tapered, giving a sweet smiling expression. The neck is short and heavy set. The rounded eyes are moderately wide set and may be gold to copper, a clear, brilliant orange being the most favored color. The ears are small, set high on the head, with slightly rounded tips.

The legs are comparatively short and surprisingly fine-boned in comparison to the hefty body. The round feet are medium sized, which makes them appear almost dainty compared with the body mass. The medium-length tail tapers to an oval tip.

The double coat is soft and lush—especially thick on the adult male—and adds bulk to the appearance of both sexes. It is medium short and slightly woolly in texture (it should open like a sheepskin at the neck and flanks). It has a resilient undercoat and a long, water-resistant topcoat. Because brushing would damage the protective undercoat, it is best to use only a comb to groom your Chartreux about once a week. At other times, simply stroke the coat frequently, running your fingers through the fur and finish with a rub over with a damp chamois.

Varieties The Chartreux comes only in blue, the soft blue-gray tones ranging from ash to slate. Each hair is tipped with silver, which gives the coat an iridescent shine. The nose leather is slate gray, the lips are blue, and the paw pads are rose-taupe.

Temperament Gentle and affectionate, the agile Chartreux makes a playful and delightful companion, but the tiny voice is a surprise in such a substantial cat. Its strength, intelligence and adaptability have enabled it to survive through centuries and these qualities should be preserved by breeders.

PET FACTS

Weekly combing

Can tolerate cool weather

Indoor and outdoor

Playful and gentle

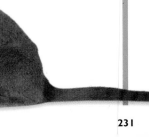

CORNISH REX

Playful and affectionate, the Cornish Rex is distinguished by its unusual wavy coat like that of the Rex rabbit, from which it derives its name. A born acrobat, lively and intelligent, it makes a fascinating pet.

blue mackerel tabby

History These highly unusual cats originated quite spontaneously, probably from a mutated gene, in Cornwall, England, as the name indicates. The first Cornish Rex appeared in a litter born in 1950 and the breed has fascinated geneticists ever since. Although several individuals sent to the US in the late 1950s were developed independently of the Cornish strain, there is no noticeable difference between the two and, in fact, the Cornish strain is still predominant in the US today. It was first accepted for championship competition in the US in 1979 and is now accepted for competition worldwide.

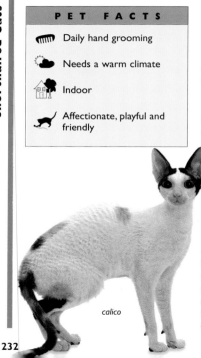

calico

Description Lean and lithe bodied, the Cornish Rex has an arched back and a tucked-up stomach, something along the lines of a whippet. Its head is oval and comparatively small and its large ears are set high on the head. The high cheekbones and high-bridged Roman nose are unmistakable distinguishing marks of the breed.

The medium-sized oval eyes are very wide set, but their color is of secondary importance and need not conform to the shade of the coat. Whatever the eye color, it should be clear and intense.

The legs are very long and slender and the cat stands high on its feet, almost as if poised on tiptoe. The paws are dainty, slightly oval, and the paw pads should harmonize with the coat color. The tail is long and flexible, with so little visible hair that it looks like a very fine whip.

The coat is most unusual. It is short, extremely soft, silky and completely free of guard hairs. Ideally, the fur lies close to the body, falling in washboard waves, like cut velvet or the fleece of Persian lamb. The curls extend from the top of the head across the back, sides and hips, continuing to the tip of the tail. The fur on the underside of the chin and on the chest and abdomen is short and noticeably wavy. When the coat is stroked lightly, it feels incredibly soft and satiny. Grooming consists of regularly stroking the coat and an occasional wipe over with a silk cloth or a damp chamois to remove dead hair. In spite of common belief to the contrary, the Cornish Rex does

black smoke

shed hair, triggering allergies in susceptible people just as other cat hair can do.

Varieties The coat of the Cornish Rex may be any color or pattern, including color-pointed. Because it is the coat that sets this breed apart from others, it is of paramount importance in show judging and most standards allot almost 50 points of the tally to the coat alone.

Temperament Although it looks wary and sophisticated, the Cornish Rex is extremely affectionate and people oriented. It is an active cat that remains kitten-like well into maturity and it can be very inventive in its play. It likes to fetch and catch, even using its paws to toss and bat small objects.

red classic tabby

233

DEVON REX

The intriguing appearance and charming personality of the Devon Rex appeals to lovers of the unusual and exotic all around the world. Although a comparatively recent arrival on the cat scene, it has already won many staunch supporters.

History Like the Cornish Rex, the English Devon Rex originated from a single kitten in the early 1960s. This spontaneous mutation sported a curly coat, but strangely enough, although the coats of the two cats are so similar, the mutant gene is not the same. The breed was accepted for championship showing in 1982 and remains remarkably unchanged from its original head type, conformation, coat and disposition. It is now bred worldwide.

Description The muscular body is small to medium sized, with a good density of muscle. For such a small animal it is surprisingly heavy. The head is comparatively small and has a modified wedge shape, with a short muzzle and prominent cheek bones.

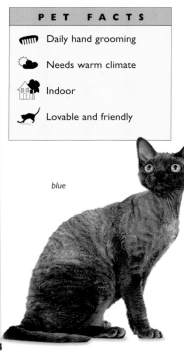

blue

chocolate silver tabby

black

The elfin face is full cheeked and the nose in profile has a strongly marked stop. Whisker pads are prominent. The strikingly large ears are very wide at the base and set very low on the sides of the head. The eartips are rounded and the ears are sometimes tufted. The oval eyes are large and wide set, sloping toward the outer edge of the ears. Their color need not harmonize with coat color.

The legs are very long and slim and the cat stands high on its small, oval feet, almost as if poised on tiptoe. The paw pads should harmonize with the coat color. A Devon Rex has a thicker tail than a Cornish Rex and it is not as whip-like. It looks thicker because the wave of the fur is looser and the tail comes to a blunt rather than pointed end.

Since the Devon Rex has less fur than most cats, it feels pleasantly warm on your lap. Although the Devon has some guard hair, the coat is not dense. The other hairs are downy soft and feel like incredibly smooth suede. The coat presents a rippled rather than tightly waved effect. The wave is most apparent when the coat is smoothed with the hand. Grooming consists of wiping over with a silk cloth or a damp chamois to remove dead hair.

Varieties The Devon Rex may come in any combination of colors and patterns, including colorpointed. Its wavy, suede-like coat is one of its distinguishing features, along with its highly prized elfin or pixie look.

Temperament Although Devons love to play, they also like to sit cozily in your lap. They show great affection, and may mature more rapidly than some other breeds. The kittens are strong and mobile at birth.

tortoiseshell

silver

PET FACTS	
🪮	Daily hand grooming
☀️	Needs warm climate
🏠	Indoor
🐈	Devoted and affectionate

EGYPTIAN MAU

Elegance and grace are the hallmarks of the Egyptian Mau. Its beautifully marked coat and well-balanced temperament recommend it as a pet and, being the only natural strain of spotted cat, it also has rarity value.

History Thought to have originated naturally in Cairo, the Egyptian Mau (mau means cat) may be a descendant of the venerated cat of ancient Egypt. The American breed is based on just three animals imported from Egyptian stock in 1956 by an exiled Russian princess, Nathalie Troubetskoy. Until recently, Egyptian Maus in the US and Canada all traced their ancestry to two of those original imports, but the gene pool has recently been broadened. The breed gained championship status in the US in 1977.

Description The graceful, muscular body of the Egyptian Mau is medium in length and size and is very strong. The head is a slightly rounded wedge, medium in length. It is not full-cheeked and the profile shows a gentle contour from the bridge of the nose to the forehead. The ears should be medium to large and somewhat pointed, continuing the planes of the head.

The rounded, almond-shaped eyes are large and alert, slanting slightly toward the ears. The color develops as the cats mature and in adults they are a vivid green.

The slender legs are in proportion to the body, with the hind legs longer than the front ones; the dainty feet are small and slightly oval. The medium-length tail tapers from a wide base, but is never whip-like.

The lustrous coat hair is medium length with a high shine. Little grooming is needed apart from a regular combing or rub over to remove dead hair.

Varieties The Mau comes in four colors: silver, bronze, smoke and black. (The black Mau is not eligible for championship showing, but can be used in a breeding program.) In silver and bronze, the hair is dense and must accommodate two or more bands of ticking. In the smoke color, the hair is fine and silky.

The silver ground color is a pale, clear silver, lighter on the underbody. Markings are black and contrast strongly with ground color. Eyes are vivid green, the paw pads are black, and the nose leather is brick red.

The bronze ground color is a pale warm bronze, with a lighter beige underbody. Markings are dark brown and contrast strongly with ground color. Eyes are a vivid green, the paw pads are dark brown and the nose leather is reddish brown.

The smoke ground color is a silvery white with jet black spots. The silvery white hairs have black tipping in the spotted areas and gray tipping in between, giving the coat a "sooty" look. Both the feet and paw pads are black, and the nose leather, lips and vivid green eyes are strongly outlined in black.

Temperament Very devoted, the Egyptian Mau is not an easy cat to transfer to a new owner. It is very intelligent and loyal and is thought to have a good memory. Active and playful, it indicates happiness by "talking" in a soft, melodious voice. The tail wiggles at great speed with joy.

smoke

bronze

EXOTIC SHORTHAIR

Blessed with a gorgeous coat that is much easier to look after than the Persian's, the Exotic Shorthair appeals to many people. Its temperament shows the best qualities of its varied ancestors, and it is also healthy and long-lived.

black smoke

blue

History Before the Exotic was recognized for championship showing in 1967, many breeders of American Shorthairs (previously called Domestic Shorthairs) broke the rules by breeding them to Persians to improve the coat. The results of these matings did far better in the show ring than true Domestic Shorthairs with full pedigrees, but the practice led to falsification of pedigrees and surprises in litters when two "shorthairs" combined to produce longhaired kittens.

Finally, the Cat Fanciers' Association was persuaded in 1967 to establish a new breed called Exotic, to legitimize the combination of such diverse breeds as Burmese, Abyssinians, American Shorthairs and Persians. In recent years, however, the only breed that can legally be used to produce Exotics is Persian, and the breed now closely resembles the Persian in every way, except in the length of the coat.

Description The Exotic is a heavily boned, well-balanced cat. Its body is stocky, low on the legs, broad and deep through the chest

brown classic tabby and white

and equally massive across the shoulders and rump, with a well-rounded midsection and level back. Although it is a medium to large cat, the quality of characteristics is more of a determining consideration than size.

The head is round and massive, with great breadth of skull. The face is round with round underlying bone structure, and is set on a short, thick neck. The nose is short, snub and broad, with a break between the eyes. The nose leather is in harmony with the coat color. The cheeks are full and the jaws broad and powerful. The brilliant eyes are large, round and full, set level and far apart. The ears are small with round tips, tilted forward and not unduly open at the base. They are set far apart and low on the head.

The legs are short, thick and strong and the forelegs are straight. The paws are large, round and firm, with pads to harmonize with the coat color. The tail is short, bushy and in proportion to the body. It is normally carried low.

The coat is dense, plush, soft and full of life, and has a rich, thick undercoat. It stands well out from the body. Although very easy to groom, this needs to be done regularly, especially when the cat is shedding its winter coat, in order to avoid hairballs. Comb with a medium-toothed comb

PET FACTS

- Regular combing
- Can tolerate cool climate
- Indoor and outdoor
- A loyal companion, quiet and playful

white

smoke tortie

blue cream

to remove dead hair and brush with a rubber brush.

Varieties The Exotic Shorthair comes in all colors and patterns, including colorpoint. Their eye color must conform to their coat color in order to be shown. These are just a few from the vast range.

Blue: light blue (lighter shades preferred) and an even tone from the nose to the tip of the tail (a solid darker shade is more acceptable than a slightly patterned lighter shade). The nose leather and paw pads are blue and the eyes are brilliant copper.

Blue-cream: blue with clearly defined patches of solid cream well broken up all over the body, legs and tail. The nose leather and paw pads are blue and/or pink and the eyes are brilliant copper.

Smoke tortie: the ground color is white with the end of each hair deeply tipped with black and red in the clearly defined patches of the tortoiseshell pattern (until it moves, the cat looks like a tortoiseshell); a blaze on the face in red is desirable. The nose leather and paw pads are brick red and/or black and the eyes are brilliant copper.

Black smoke: the ground color is white with the end of each hair deeply tipped with black (until it

cream point

moves, the cat looks solid black). The points and mask are black with only a narrow band of white on each hair near the skin. Nose leather and paw pads are copper.

White: pure white fur with no shading or marking and no black hairs. The nose leather and paw pads are pink and the eyes are brilliant copper, blue or odd-eyed (one blue and one copper).

Chocolate: warm, medium to dark chocolate coat, even in color with no shading, markings or white hairs. The eye rims, nose leather and paw pads are chocolate and the eyes are brilliant copper.

Red tabby: the ground color is light red with rich, vibrant, mahogany red markings. The nose leather and paw pads are brick red to salmon pink and the eyes are brilliant copper.

Brown tabby and white: ground color, including lips and chin, is a rich tawny brown. Markings are black and the nose leather is brick red outlined with chocolate. The paw pads are deep brown to black and the eyes are copper. Some associations require that the white portion comprises at least one third of the cat and includes an inverted "V" on the face. Others allow any proportion of brown tabby and white, with no preference given to the amount of white or lack thereof.

Tortie and white (calico): the coat is white with patches of red and black distributed in any proportion. The eyes are copper. The red and black may also be in a chinchilla,

red tabby

shaded, smoke or torbie pattern. Calicos also come in blue cream (called dilute calico by some), lilac cream or chocolate cream.

Colorpoint: points and mask are darker than the ground color, but are in harmonious shades, and the nose leather and paw pads conform to the point color. The eyes are blue.

Temperament The Exotic has a lively, friendly, lovable nature and seldom makes a sound. It is a sweet and loyal companion, easy to live with and very affectionate.

241

HAVANA BROWN

The picture of feline grace, the Havana Brown is a gentle creature, rather shy but very loving to its owner. Breeders worked long and hard to achieve this all-brown cat, the challenge being met in different ways in Britain and the US.

History Although breeders had been trying since the 1890s to develop an all-brown cat, it wasn't until the early 1950s that crosses in Britain between a seal point Siamese and a black shorthaired cat with Siamese forebears produced the desired result. These cats, previously known as Chestnut Brown Foreigns, are the Havana Brown's foundation stock, but subsequent development in Britain and the US took different paths. The first Chestnut Brown Foreigns were obtained by American breeders in the mid-1950s and the Havana Brown descended from those animals is now a much sturdier cat than its British counterpart. The Havana Brown was recognized for championship competition in Britain in 1958 and in the US in 1959.

Description These cats differ markedly in body type in the US, Britain and other countries. In the US, the Havana (pictured) has a moderate-sized, well-muscled body, striking a balance between the cobbiness of the Exotic Shorthair and the svelte length of the Siamese. The head is angular, longer than it is wide and in profile has a distinct nose break. The head of the English Havana is more like that of a

Siamese. The head is longer than it is wide, narrowing to a rounded muzzle with a pronounced break on both sides behind the whisker pads. The somewhat narrow muzzle and whisker break are distinctive characteristics and must appear in all show specimens. When viewed in profile, there is an obvious stop at the eyes and the end of the muzzle appears almost square, making the profile quite unmistakable.

The oval eyes are set wide apart and there should be no squinting. They are brilliant and expressive, in a vivid shade of mid-green. The eye color develops slowly as the animal matures, and deeper shades are preferred. The ears are large with rounded tips, and they tilt forward.

The legs are relatively long compared to the body, the legs of females being slim and dainty; the slenderness and length of leg will be less evident in a more powerfully muscled, mature male. The oval paws are compact and have either brown or rose-pink pads.

The short to medium-length coat is smooth, lustrous and needs only to be combed about twice a week with a fine-toothed comb. To bring up the gloss, simply rub a damp chamois over the coat.

Varieties The Havana Brown comes in only one color, brown. It is best described as a rich and even shade of warm mahogany throughout—the color tends toward red rather than black. The coat should be free of tabby markings and the whiskers must also be brown. The nose leather is brown with a rosy flush.

Temperament From their mixed ancestry, these cats have picked up a grab-bag of traits to charm their owners. They are very curious and characteristically use their paws to investigate, touching and feeling anything that intrigues them. They are people oriented

PET FACTS

Twice weekly

Warm climate

Indoor

Quiet and affectionate

red and white
bicolor

PET FACTS

🐾 Daily combing or brushing

☀ Warm climate

🏡 Indoor

🐈 Intelligent, active
and talkative

JAPANESE BOBTAIL

Familiar to travelers as the cat with the raised paw in the china figurines sold in Japan as good luck symbols, the Japanese Bobtail is distinguished by its unusual short tail. This is preferably carried upright like a pompom.

History Although the breed has existed in Japan for many centuries, it was unknown in the US until 1968, when Elizabeth Freret imported the first three Japanese Bobtails from Japan.

Breed standards were agreed on in the 1970s and the Bobtail was granted championship status in 1976. At that time, it was known only as a shorthair, but a longhaired version was accepted for showing in 1993.

Description The medium-sized body is long, lean and elegant, but not tubular like the Siamese. The head is long and finely chiseled and forms a perfect equilateral triangle with gentle curving lines, high cheekbones and a noticeable whisker break. The nose is long with a gentle dip at or just below eye level. The large oval eyes are wide set and alert, but their color does not necessarily conform to the color of the coat. The ears are large, upright and have rounded tips. They are set wide apart so as to continue the lines of the triangular head.

The legs are long and slender with the deeply bent hind legs longer than the front. The hind legs are naturally bent when the cat is standing

black and white

more curves, angles or kinks, or any combination of these.

The shorthair Japanese Bobtail has a medium-length coat that is soft and silky, with no noticeable undercoat. The longhair has a soft, silky, medium to long coat that lies flat and follows the lines of the body. There is minimal shedding. A ruff is desirable, as are ear and toe tufts. Needs only brushing with a soft bristle brush or a light combing.

Varieties The Japanese Bobtail comes in all colors, except solid lilac, chocolate and colorpointed. The most popular color is called "Mi-ke" (mee-kay), which is white with red and black splotches, identical to what is called calico in the West. Another popular pattern is the bicolor. This is a white cat with one other color, either solid or patterned. If there are no more than two spots of color on the body, it is referred to as a van pattern. If there are more than two spots, it is called a bicolor.

relaxed. The paws are oval with pads in a color that suits the coat. Each individual has its own variation of the unusual short tail, which is carried upright or close to the body curled like a pompom. The tail may be flexible or rigid, in harmony with the rest of the cat's body. It must be clearly visible and comprise one or

Temperament Active, intelligent and talkative, the Japanese Bobtail has a lively and vivacious charm. Its voice is soft and it usually responds when spoken to. It is friendly, very adaptable, and loves children.

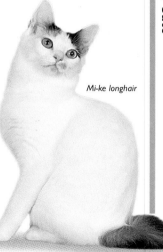
Mi-ke longhair

KORAT

With a winning combination of silver-blue fur tipped with silver, and large, luminous green eyes, who would argue at the Korat being called lucky? Certainly nobody in Thailand, where the breed has been esteemed for centuries.

History Although found in all parts of Thailand, the Korat takes its name from one particular province. The earliest picture of this elegant cat, also known as the Si-Sawat, was found in a book of paintings in Bangkok's National Library. It is believed to have been painted during the Ayudhya Period of Siamese History (1350-1767).

When the first pair, Nara and Darra, arrived in the US in 1959, the Korat's blue coat was spotted with white and the tail was kinked, both considered unacceptable traits for showing. These defects have now been bred out and Korats were accepted for championship status in the US in 1966 and in Britain in 1975.

Description The muscular, supple body of the Korat is semi-cobby, neither compact nor svelte, with males being heavier than females. Chest is broad and back curved.

The head is heart-shaped and very broad across the eyes, unlike any other breed. The eyebrow ridges form the upper curves of the heart and the sides of the face curve gently down to the chin to complete this attractive shape. The chin and jaw are strong and well-developed.

In profile, the nose has a downward curve just above the leather, which is dark blue or lavender. The large ears have rounded tips, a wide flare at the base, and are set high on the head, giving an impression of alertness.

The prominent eyes are large and luminous green with extraordinary depth and brilliance. They may be yellow or amber with a green tinge around the pupil in young animals, but change color as the cat matures. It may take up to four years before the green is fully developed. The eyes are well-rounded when fully open, and slightly slanted when closed or partly closed.

The slender legs should be in good proportion to the body, the front legs being shorter than the back. The paws are oval with pinkish lavender pads, and the medium-length tail has a rounded tip. Some associations allow a kink in the tail (which can be felt but is not visible).

The short, single coat is glossy and fine, lying close to the body. The coat is inclined to part, or "break," over the spine as the cat moves. Regular combing will remove dead hair and minimize the possibility of hairballs forming. For a glossy shine, wipe over with a silk cloth or damp chamois.

Varieties The Korat comes only in blue. The coat is a solid silvery blue, each hair being tipped with enough silver to produce a halo effect. Where the coat is short, the silver shine is intensified. There should be no tabby markings.

Temperament These gentle cats love to romp, but dislike loud, sudden noises. They are calm and sweet-natured and enjoy human company, particularly children, and love to be stroked and petted. Their senses of sight, smell and hearing are thought to be unusually acute and they are excellent hunters.

PET FACTS

- Daily hand grooming
- Warm climate
- Indoor and outdoor
- Affectionate and playful

PET FACTS

🐾 Daily combing, especially longhairs

☀☁ Can tolerate cool climate

🏠🌳 Indoor and outdoor

🐈 Intelligent and courageous

brown patched mackerel tabby kitten

MANX

The long-lived Manx is famous for having no tail, although many do have vestiges, and for being the symbol of the Isle of Man. It comes in almost every color and pattern imaginable and makes a charming family pet.

History The Manx cat originated on the Isle of Man, off the coast of England in the Irish Sea. The isolation of the island probably perpetuated the tailless trait in these cats, although legend supplies far more fanciful explanations. Manx cats still abound on the island. Although the Manx was a popular and well-established breed in Britain before the birth of the cat fancy in the 1870s, it is no longer accepted for competition in shows sponsored there. The objection is that breeding this cat will perpetuate a lethal spine defect. It is accepted for showing in the US and has been popular there since about 1930.

Description The Manx has the shortest body of any of the breeds. The chest is broad and the short back arches from the shoulders to the round rump. The head is round but slightly longer than it is wide, with prominent cheeks and a jowly appearance. In profile, there is a gentle dip in the nose. The nose leather should harmonize with the coat. The muzzle is slightly longer than it is wide with a definite whisker break and large, round whisker pads. The neck is short and thick. The large eyes are round and full and set at a slight angle toward the nose. Eye color does not necessarily conform to coat color. The medium-sized ears are wide at the base, tapering gradually to a

red mackerel tabby longhair

rounded tip and set far apart.

The hind legs are muscular and well boned and longer than the forelegs, which are short and set well apart, emphasizing the broad, deep chest. The rump sits considerably higher than the shoulders. The paws are round and the pad color should harmonize with the coat.

Show specimens have no tail, but these are rare. Anyone interested in breeding Manx should be aware of the risks and high mortality rate of kittens. In fact, the last vertebra of the spine is missing, which results in a dip or hollow at the base of the spine where that bone would normally be. Handle such a cat with care—never pat the rump roughly as most Manx are chronically sensitive in that area. In spite of the spinal abnormality, the Manx is a speedy and powerful runner.

The double coat is short and thick. In the longhaired version, also called the Cymric, the double coat is soft and silky, full and plush, falling smoothly over the body. Groom both types often by gently brushing or combing with a medium-toothed comb. This will remove dead hair and prevent matting.

Varieties The Manx comes in any color or pattern, including color-pointed, bicolor, solid and tabby.

Temperament The playful Manx loves to perch on the highest possible point, even indoors. It will retrieve and bury toys as a dog does.

black and white bicolor

red classic tabby

PET FACTS

- Daily grooming
- Cool or warm climate, depending on coat length
- Indoor only
- Varies with ancestry

MUNCHKIN

For those who must have the very latest, no breed is more up to the minute than the Munchkin. Admirers of this short-legged charmer, as yet not widely recognized, are confident it has a big future.

History Cats with short legs are not new to science, although they have only recently been discovered by the cat fancy. In a 1944 edition of the *Veterinary Record*, Dr. H. E. Williams-Jones described four generations of cats with short limbs. The cats' movements were listed as being ferret-like. Unfortunately, these cats seemed to disappear during World War II, as did the bloodlines of many purebred cats. The Munchkin appeared spontaneously in Louisiana in the 1980s. From a pregnant black female found by Sandra Hochenedel in 1983, several colonies have now been established. These currently span multiple generations.

tortie and white

Description At the present time, the Munchkin appears to come in every sort of body type, head type and coat length. The only thing these cats have in common is their extremely short legs. Since the gene pool is unlimited, there are no clear guidelines as to what type the Munchkin will ultimately resemble. Some Munchkin breeders are mating to Persians, others to Siamese and still others to Abyssinians. At present, it is not possible to present a picture of the ultimate type, apart from its distinctively short legs.

In the studies that have been conducted so far, no unforeseen skeletal changes have been associated with the short-legged gene and there is no evidence to suggest that these cats have any of the back problems of short-legged dogs, such as the Dachshund. This is undoubtedly because the cat spine differs markedly from that of the dog in its construction and flexibility, and spinal problems are rare in cats. What the Munchkin does have in common with short-legged dogs is that the front legs are bowed. This does not seem to affect its climbing ability, but its jumping ability is limited by the shortness of the hind legs, making it difficult for these cats to escape danger.

At present, this breed is accepted for championship competition in

odd-eyed white longhair

only one of the US associations, The International Cat Association (TICA). The other associations have adopted a wait-and-see attitude for two reasons. One is to rule out the possibility of the shortened legs causing health problems in the cats in later life. The other is that because there is such wide disparity in type as a result of outcrosses to so many other breeds, it is difficult to set a type standard. Munchkin fanciers are confident that the eventual outcome will be a happy one for both them and the breed.

seal point

Varieties At present, the Munchkin can have any type of head, body, coat or color. The only feature identifying it as a Munchkin is its short legs.

Temperament Since the Munchkin has so many different ancestors, its temperament will depend largely upon which cats are on its pedigree. As with any cat, the conditions under which it is raised and the amount of attention given during kittenhood are also factors in the temperament.

OCICAT

A relatively recent arrival on the show scene, the spectacular spotted Ocicat has the beauty and athleticism of the wild cat with the disposition of the domestic cat. This appealing animal is a perfect choice for a family.

chocolate

History The first Ocicat appeared unexpectedly in a litter from a crossing of a ruddy Abyssinian with a seal point Siamese. This kitten eventually matured to a large, ivory cat with bright golden spots and copper eyes. The Michigan breeder, Virginia Daly, named the cat Tonga, but Daly's daughter called Tonga an Ocicat because of his resemblance to an ocelot. After Tonga's birth in 1964, other breeders followed the same crossing to develop more of the intriguing Ocicats. Later the American Shorthair was added to the mix to broaden the genetic base. The Ocicat was accepted for championship competition in 1986.

Description The medium to large Ocicat has a rather long, well-muscled body that is solid and hard. It should look athletic and lithe, not bulky or coarse.

The head is a modified wedge and there is a gentle rise, in profile, from the bridge of the nose to the brow. The broad muzzle finishes with a suggestion of squareness and the chin is strong. The neck is gracefully arched. The large eyes are almond shaped and are angled slightly up toward the ears. The moderately large ears are wide set and continue the outward lines of the face; they are neither flared nor upright.

The medium-long legs are well muscled, with oval feet. The tail is fairly long, slim and tapered, and tipped at the end with a dark color.

The coat is short, smooth and satiny in texture with a lustrous shine. It is tight and close lying and there should be no suggestion of woolliness. All the hairs are ticked in a banded pattern, except the tip of

cinnamon

Varieties The Ocicat comes with spots in an array of eye-catching colors: tawny (brown-spotted tabby), chocolate, cinnamon, blue, lavender, fawn, silver, chocolate silver, cinnamon silver, blue silver, lavender silver and fawn silver. The ground colors range from white to ivory to bronze. All eye colors are accepted, except blue, and there is no correlation between the eye color and coat color.

the tail, which is solid. The forehead is marked with an intricate tabby "M" extending up over the head and breaking into small spots on the lower neck and shoulders.

Rows of round spots run along the spine from the shoulder blades to the tail. Spots sprinkle the shoulders and hind-quarters, and extend down the legs. The belly is also well spotted and the eyes are ringed with mascara markings. Very little grooming is necessary, beyond regular hand grooming and an occasional brushing.

PET FACTS	
🪮	Daily hand grooming
☁	Warm climate only
🏠	Indoor
🐈	Easily trained and very affectionate

Temperament Because of its Siamese, Abyssinian and American Shorthair ancestors, it exhibits some of the qualities of all three. It becomes very attached to the people in its family but is not demanding. It does well in a household with other cats or dogs and is usually extroverted and friendly with strangers, bright and easily trained. Being very sociable, it doesn't like to be left alone for long periods.

blue

253

white longhair

ORIENTAL SHORTHAIR

A comparatively recent development, Oriental Shorthairs already run the gamut of colors and patterns. Their sleek lines, intelligence and extroverted personalities come largely from the foundation of Siamese on which they were built.

ebony ticked tabby

History In the 1950s, a British cat fancier created a brown shorthair with green eyes and a Siamese body. Photographs of two such kittens appeared in the August 1954 issue of the British journal *Our Cats.* At first the chestnut brown kittens were called Havanas, according to some authorities, after the rabbit of the same color. Others say they were named after Havana tobacco. When the Governing Council of the Cat Fancy in Britain recognized these chestnut brown cats for championship competition in 1958, the name Chestnut Brown Foreign was chosen for the breed. In 1962, another British breeder and geneticist began working to produce a blue-eyed white cat of the same foreign type. These cats were not deaf, as some other blue-eyed cats are, and they were accorded championship status in Britain under the name Foreign White.

Peter and Vickie Markstein, two of the better-known Siamese breeders in the US, were so taken with the Foreign Whites and similar cats that in 1972, they decided to seek acceptance in the US for all Foreign

Shorthairs as one breed, to be called the Oriental Shorthair. The foundation stock for the Oriental Shorthair was the Siamese, from which comes the body type, plus American Shorthairs and Abyssinians, from which come the colors and patterns. The Oriental Shorthair was first accepted for championship competition in the US in 1977 and all the other US registries have since followed suit. In other countries, these cats are slightly smaller and are regarded as separate breeds called Orientals or Foreigns of various colors.

Description The body is like that of the Siamese, sleek, slender and refined in every respect. The medium-sized torso is graceful, long and svelte, combining fine bones and firm muscles. The shoulders and hips continue the tubular lines and the hips are never wider than the shoulders. The abdomen is tight and firm. The head is a long,

tapering wedge, starting at the nose and flaring out in straight lines to the tips of the ears to form a triangle, with no break at the whiskers. The muzzle is fine and wedge-shaped. The tip of the chin lines up with the tip of the nose in the same vertical

ebony

plane, neither receding nor excessively massive. Nose leather should harmonize with the coat color.

The almond-shaped eyes are medium size and slant upward from the nose, following the line of the head and ears. They should not be crossed and any hint of a crossed eye is grounds for disqualification on the show bench. The eyes are usually green, but white Orientals may have blue, green or odd eyes (one blue and one green). Ears are strikingly large and pointed, and open at the base. The legs are long and slim with dainty, small, oval paws. The paw pads should harmonize with the coat color. The long, thin tail tapers to a fine point and has no kinks.

The Oriental comes in both shorthair and longhair varieties. The short, fine coat of the Oriental Shorthair is glossy and lies close to body. An occasional combing to remove dead hair and a wipe over with a damp chamois to make the coat gleam are all that are needed by

blue ticked tabby longhair

way of grooming. The medium-length coat of the Oriental Longhair is fine and silky with no downy undercoat. It lies close to the body, except on the tail, which is long and feathery. More frequent combing is necessary to keep this type of coat in good condition.

Varieties Both shorthair and longhair varieties come in many patterns and more than 300 colors. These include the normal solid colors, as well as chestnut, lavender, cinnamon and fawn, plus tabby patterns and spotted coats. With the addition of the silver gene, they also come in smokes of all colors. It would not be possible to list all the color combinations, but a few of the most popular are:

White: pure white, with pale pink nose leather, dark pink paw pads and sapphire eyes.

Blue: even blue right to the root of each hair, lighter shades preferred in the US, with blue nose leather and paw pads and green eyes.

Ebony: pure jet black right to the root of each hair, with black nose leather, black or brown paw pads and emerald eyes.

Silver tabby: silver background with dense black markings, black or brick red nose leather rimmed with black, black paw pads and green eyes.

Lavender tabby (lilac in Britain): beige background with lavender gray markings, faded lavender or pink nose leather rimmed with lavender-gray, faded lavender paw pads and green eyes.

Red ticked tabby: bright apricot background with deep rich red markings, each hair is ticked with shades of apricot and red, pink or pink rimmed with red nose leather and blue paw pads. Green eyes are preferred in the US, green to copper in Britain. The face, legs and tail

red ticked tabby

lavender tabby

must show distinct tabby striping and there should be at least one distinct necklace.

Ebony ticked tabby (brown in Britain): warm coppery brown background with dense black markings, each hair ticked with shades of brown and black, black nose leather or pink rimmed with black, brown or black paw pads, eyes may be rimmed with black and green is the preferred color. The face, legs and tail must show distinct tabby striping and there should be at least one distinct necklace.

Chestnut spotted: warm coppery brown background shading to creamy ivory on the undersides, with clearly defined markings of dark brown in a classic tabby pattern on the head and numerous round or oval spots on the back and legs, spots or broken rings on the tail, brick red nose leather, black or dark brown paw pads and green eyes.

Smoke: pure white undercoat with the hair of the top coat tipped in one or more darker colors, the nose leather and paw pads are in keeping with the contrast color and green eyes. Any color is possible as the contrast color.

With such a tremendous range of possibilities, it is no wonder that these cats are becoming so popular worldwide. The only limit seems to be the imagination of the breeders.

Temperament Oriental cats are intelligent, gentle and love company. They dislike being left alone and can be mischievous if bored and lonely. They will do anything to get your attention and remain playful, high-spirited and affectionate well into maturity. The queens have large litters and are careful and loving mothers. The kittens don't change color as they mature as Siamese kittens do.

white

RUSSIAN BLUE

Handsome, gentle and sweet natured, the Russian Blue
is in every way a classic. Its elegant lines, astonishingly
rich coat and striking green eyes always turn heads and,
added to all that, it is healthy and easy to look after.

*four-month-old
kitten*

History The breed seems to have
originated in the most northerly
regions of Russia and Scandinavia
and went by a variety of names,
including Archangel cats, Foreign
blues, Spanish cats and Maltese cats,
the reasons for which have long been
forgotten. The Maltese cat label
persisted in the US until early this
century. A Russian Blue competed in
Britain in 1875 in a class for all-blue
cats of all types, but it was not until
1912 that the breed was separated
into a class of its own.

Little work was done with the
Russian Blue until after World
War II, when American breeders
combined the British bloodlines,
with their plush, silvery coats,

with Scandinavian strains, with their
emerald-green eyes and flat profiles.
The flat profiles came from crosses of
a blue cat from Finland with a blue
point Siamese.

Description The lithe, slender and
graceful Russian Blue has a fine-
boned body that is firm, muscular
and long, but not tubular. The head
is a medium wedge, neither long and
tapering nor short and massive. The
muzzle is blunt and part of the total
wedge. The top of the skull is long
and flat in profile, gently descending
to slightly above the eyes and
continuing at a slight downward

angle in a straight line to the tip of the nose. The nose leather is slate gray in the US and blue in the Britain. There is no nose break or stop, but the thick fur of some animals makes it seem that there is a slight dip in the nose when light is reflected off the silver tipping. The face is broad. The wide-set eyes are rounded and vivid green and the wide-set ears are rather large and broad at the base, with tips more pointed than rounded, and with a slight flare.

The fine-boned legs are long and the paws small and slightly rounded with pads of lavender pink or mauve in the US and blue in Britain. The tapered tail is long and in proportion to the body. The double coat is short, dense, fine and plush, like seal fur. No other cat has a coat quite like it. It stands out from the body and has a distinctive soft and silky feel. The ideal coat will hold the imprint of your fingers as you run them through it. Grooming entails regular hand grooming and an occasional combing or a rub with a damp chamois to bring up the luster.

Varieties The Russian Blue is shown only in blue. Lighter shades are preferred and the color should be even and bright throughout and free from tabby markings. The guard hairs are distinctly tipped with silver, giving the cat a lustrous, silvery shine.

Temperament Docile and affectionate, the Russian Blue quickly becomes devoted to its loved ones. It is gentle, playful and a good companion. Although somewhat shy, it gets along well with children and other pets. It is very intelligent and likes to open doors and fetch. It has a quiet, almost musical little voice.

PET FACTS	
🪮	Daily hand grooming
☁️	Can tolerate cool climate
🌳	Indoor and outdoor
🐈	Undemanding, intelligent and affectionate

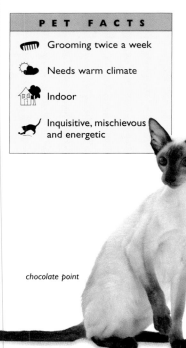

chocolate point

PET FACTS
Grooming twice a week
Needs warm climate
Indoor
Inquisitive, mischievous and energetic

SIAMESE

A gift fit for a king, the Siamese cat is a true aristocrat, with elegant lines and beautiful coloring. It can, however, be rowdy and boisterous, and it is perhaps this contradiction that makes the breed universally popular.

History The original Siamese cats, which are still to be found in Thailand, bear little or no resemblance to today's show types. They have stocky bodies, rounded heads, crossed eyes and kinked tails, all of which would disqualify them from competition today. In its native land, the Siamese was nurtured and protected within the temple and palace walls for centuries, and featured prominently in art and literature.

The breed became known to the rest of the world when the royal family of Siam (now Thailand) presented them as gifts to visiting dignitaries. This was considered a great honor because the cats belonged exclusively to royalty.

The Siamese began appearing in British cat shows in the late nineteenth century and in America in the early part of this century. The only accepted color was seal point, and when blue points were introduced in 1934, some judges were so opposed to this new color that they refused to judge them as a separate class, which caused great consternation. The next color to be recognized, in 1946, was the chocolate point. This color resulted from a daughter of Wong Mau, the original Burmese imported into the

red point

US, being mated to a Siamese. In 1955, the lilac point (also known as the frost point) was recognized. These four colors prevailed for a number of years until the breeders of red points, tortie points and lynx points began to clamor for recognition of their colors. The cat fancy was divided about whether to accept these latest colors.

Debate raged, sometimes quite heatedly. As a result, some associations accepted red, tortie and lynx points as Siamese. Others accepted them as a separate breed called Colorpoint Shorthairs.

Description The ideal Siamese is sleek, slender and refined in every respect. Its medium-sized body is graceful, long and svelte, combining fine bones and firm muscles. The shoulders and hips continue the tubular lines and the hips are never wider than the shoulders. The abdomen is tight and firm.

The head is a long, tapering wedge, starting at the nose and flaring out in straight lines to the tips of the ears to form a triangle, with no break at the whiskers. The muzzle is fine and wedge-shaped. The tip of the chin lines up with the tip of the nose in the same vertical plane, neither receding nor excessively massive. The almond-shaped eyes are medium sized and slant upward from the nose, following the line of the head and ears. They should not be crossed and

blue point

lilac point

seal tortie point

any hint of a crossed eye is grounds for disqualification on the show bench. They are always brilliant sapphire blue, with deeper and more vivid shades being preferred. The ears are large, pointed and open at the base. The legs are long and slim with dainty, small, oval paws. The long, thin tail tapers to a fine point and has no kinks.

All Siamese are shorthaired, but some associations now refer to the Balinese as a longhaired Siamese. The Siamese coat is short, fine-textured and glossy, and lies close to the body. It can look as if it is "painted on." Grooming is minimal. Combing and brushing twice a week to remove dead hair will suffice. To make the coat gleam, wipe it over with a damp chamois.

Varieties Siamese are colorpoint cats and come in seal point, blue point, chocolate point, lilac point, red point, tortie point and lynx point. (The last three are

seal point kitten   *chocolate point kitten*

called Colorpoint Shorthairs in the Cat Fanciers' Association.) The tortie and lynx points also come in lilac, blue, chocolate and seal. All Siamese are pure white at birth. The color-points on the face, ears, tail, feet and legs appear as the kittens mature.

Seal point: the body is an even warm cream, darker on the back and lighter on the stomach and chest; the points are seal brown; the nose leather and paw pads are seal brown.

Blue point: the body is an even

blue cream point

bluish white with a warmer tone on the stomach and chest; points, nose leather and paw pads are slate blue.

Chocolate point: the body is an even warm ivory all over; points are warm milk chocolate; nose leather and paw pads are a cinnamon pink.

Lilac point: the body is glacial white (US) or magnolia (Britain) all over; points are frosty gray with a pink or lilac tone; the nose leather and paw pads are lavender pink.

Red point: the body is pure white, shaded with the color of the points; the points are apricot to deep red, with the deeper shades preferred; the nose leather and paw pads are flesh or coral pink.

Tortie point: the colors of the coat, nose leather and paw pads are as above for seal, blue, chocolate and lilac points, but within the color is a tabby pattern. Irregular patches of red and/or cream on the points; red and/or cream mottling on the ears and tail is permitted.

Lynx point: the colors of the coat, nose leather and paw pads are as above for seal, blue, chocolate and lilac points, but within the color is a striped pattern.

Temperament The Siamese is intelligent and lovable. It will continually amuse you with its antics while occasionally frustrating you with its ability to open seemingly locked cupboards and doors. It is a people cat and demands attention— the Siamese hates to be ignored or left by itself, and can be mischievous if bored or lonely. These cats communicate like no other. The voice of the Siamese is legendary—a female in season sounds exactly like a baby wailing for its mother and can be easily heard a block away. One of the more highly strung breeds, agile and active and seeming to be in perpetual motion, it is not the cat for everyone. But for those who take this boisterous cat into their home, the reward is boundless affection and hours of entertainment.

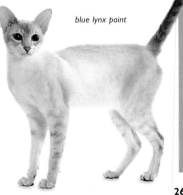

blue lynx point

263

SINGAPURA

Small and beautifully proportioned, the Singapura is a recent arrival on the US show scene and its rarity has perhaps enhanced the myths that surround it. It is an extremely pretty cat that enjoys wide appeal.

adult with kittens

History While its origin remains shrouded in mystery, the foundation stock of all Singapuras in the US is just four cats belonging to a single American breeder. They are reputed to have a connection with Singapore street cats, but this is far from certain. Whatever the truth, the gene pool is small and the future of these cats is questionable.

The breed is being developed in the US and it was first accorded championship status in 1988. It then went on to win 22 grand championship titles in its second season of showing, an amazing success.

Description This is a small cat with a delicate coloring unlike any other breed. It has a moderately stocky, muscular body, and when the animal is standing, the body, legs and floor form a square. The neck is short and thick and the head is rounded with a blunt, medium-short nose. There is a definite whisker break. In profile, there is a slight stop well below eye level; the nose then continues in a straight line to the chin. The nose leather is salmon pink, outlined with dark brown. The large, almond-shaped eyes are held wide open and are outlined with dark brown. They slant slightly upward at the outside end. No eye color except hazel, green or yellow is permitted. Brilliance is preferred and small eyes are a serious fault. The ears are large and slightly pointed, wide open at the base and deeply cupped. They should have a definite covering of light hair inside. Small ears are considered a serious fault.

The legs are heavy and well-muscled and taper to small, short oval feet and the paw pads are rosy brown. The tail, darker than the rest of the coat, is slender but not whip-like and has a blunt tip. It should have no kinks.

The sleek, silky coat feels like satin. It is fine, very short, and lies very close to the body—a springy coat is a fault. It needs very little grooming beyond an occasional combing. The sepia coat color is unique. The ground color is old ivory, with each hair on the back, top of the head, and flanks ticked with at least two bands of a deep brown separated by bands of warm old ivory (this is also known as agouti ticking). The underside of the body is a lighter shade, something like unbleached muslin.

Varieties The Singapura comes only as a shorthair and only in sepia, with ticked fur.

Temperament Active, curious and quietly affectionate, the Singapura loves to be with people. It remains interactive and playful even when fully grown and gets along very well with other animals. It is a speedy and effective hunter and the queens are noted for being especially loving and maternal.

PET FACTS	
🪮	Occasional combing
⛅	Needs a warm climate
🏡	Indoor
🐈	Affectionate and playful

seal point

PET FACTS

🪮 Occasional combing

☀️ Warm climate

🏠 Indoor

🐈 Active, playful, outgoing and affectionate

SNOWSHOE

While still comparatively rare, this hybrid of the Siamese and the bicolor American Shorthair has all the good points of its forebears. The prettily marked Snowshoe is lively, affectionate and very responsive to humans.

blue point

History Seal points and blue points with white boots, throats and facial markings have occurred spontaneously for decades. But one group of dedicated breeders in the US was so taken with the distinctive white patterning of such kittens, that they worked for years from the late 1960s to set a standard and to have these cats accepted as a new breed, which they called the Snowshoe.

This cat is the result of crossings of Siamese, Birman and bicolor American Shorthairs. It was registered by the Cat Fanciers'

Federation and the American Cat Association by 1974 and gained championship status in 1982, but not all associations recognize it for championship status as yet.

Description The Snowshoe combines the heftiness of its domestic Shorthair ancestors with the body length of its oriental ancestors. It has an athletic appearance of great power and agility, like a runner. The medium-sized body is rectangular, well muscled, powerful and heavily built. The neck should be of medium length. The head is a slightly rounded triangular wedge, with cheekbones set high. The medium-length nose is straight with a slight rise on the bridge. The nose leather varies with coat color. The large, round eyes are a vivid blue and should slant up from the nose toward the base of each ear. The medium-sized ears are slightly rounded at the tips and set forward from the outside of the head giving a continuing line from head to ears.

The strong, well-muscled legs should be of good length, in proportion to the body and well boned, but not as heavy as those of the American Shorthair. The medium-length tail should taper to a point.

The glossy coat is short to medium length and should not be double or plush. The ideal pattern, which is quite a challenge to produce, calls for a solid color on the back and sides of the animal with white confined to the insides of the legs and belly. A white throat is desirable as is white underneath the lower jaw.

The preferred facial pattern is a white muzzle in the shape of an inverted "V." Preferred foot markings are matching white boots extending to the bend of the ankle on the front feet, and matching white boots extending to just below the hock on the back feet. An occasional combing will remove any dead hair.

Varieties Preference is for cats displaying the proper amount of white and in the preferred pattern. Only two colors are allowed— seal point or blue point. The nose leather and paw pads may be either pink or the color of the points or a combination of the two.

Temperament Lively and adaptable, the Snowshoe combines the best characteristics of its American Shorthair, Birman and Siamese ancestors, and is an excellent hunter. It is full of fun, a good companion and gets along well with other animals.

seal point

seal point

SPHYNX

There seem to be no in-betweens with this cat—because of its appearance people either love it or hate it. One thing not in dispute, though, is that the Sphynx is the most unusual of cats. It is also very intelligent with a playful and affectionate nature.

black and white kittens

brown mackerel torbie

History In the early 1900s, a cat resembling a modern-day Sphynx was exhibited as the New Mexican Hairless cat. Efforts to gain recognition for this breed were not made until hairless cats appeared in Ontario, Canada, in the 1960s. In 1970, it was granted provisional status by the Cat Fanciers' Association (CFA), but progressed no further because the CFA board was concerned that the breed might have genetic problems.

The breed is currently accepted in the US by only two of the associations —the American Cat Association and The International Cat Association.

Breeders of today's Sphynx claim that in the cats now being bred there are no genetic flaws, but the cat is rarely seen outside the US. Because of its lack of insulation, it needs to eat a little more than average to maintain optimum body temperature.

Description The medium-length body is very sturdy and rounded, thick through the abdomen, with the appearance of having a full belly, but not fat. The chest is broad and barrel-shaped. The head is slightly longer than it is wide with prominent cheekbones and a slight but definite whisker break. In profile there is a distinct stop at the bridge of the nose, and the nose is covered with velvety fur. The neck is long and slender. The large eyes are deep-set and slant up toward the outer edge of the ear. Any eye color is acceptable and it need not conform to coat color. The ears are very large, wide at the base and open, with no interior hair. They are neither low-set nor on top of the head, but upright.

The long, slender legs feel firm and muscular, but are not fine boned. The neat oval paws have long slender toes. Pad color is in keeping with the coat. The tail is long, hard and tapered, with no kinks.

Despite appearances, the Sphynx is not really hairless. The skin is covered with very short, fine down that is almost imperceptible to both the eye and the hand. It should feel like soft suede. On the points (ears, muzzle, tail and feet) there is short, tightly packed soft hair. Lack of an insulating coat means that the cat feels quite warm when you touch it.

Whiskers and eyebrows may be present, either whole or broken, or there may be none. The skin often has a wrinkled appearance, especially in kittens. Because these cats sweat, a most unusual trait, they should be sponged over daily with a damp sponge to remove oils.

Varieties All Sphynx must conform to the coat description above. They can be any color and pattern, including colorpoint. Because of the invisibility of the hair, the pattern and color seem almost to be tatooed on the skin.

Temperament The Sphynx exudes quiet contentment. It has a surprising, mystical effect on anyone holding it for the first time, almost as if it casts a spell over the person.

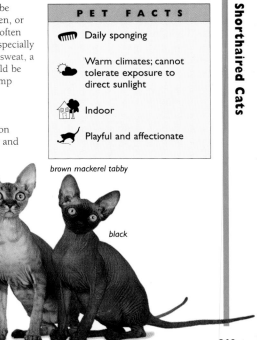

PET FACTS	
🐾	Daily sponging
☁	Warm climates; cannot tolerate exposure to direct sunlight
🏠	Indoor
🐱	Playful and affectionate

brown mackerel tabby

black

269

PET FACTS

🪮 Occasional combing

☁️ Needs warm climate

🏡 Indoor

🐈 Inquisitive, active, loving and responsive

TONKINESE

Beautiful soft colors characterize the luxurious coat of the Tonkinese, a cat with some of the best qualities of each of its parent breeds. The result of clever breeding, this lovely cat certainly justifies the effort made to create it.

History The only breed to originate in Canada, the Tonkinese was developed in the early 1960s by crossing a seal point Siamese and a sable Burmese. Feeling that Siamese show types were becoming too stylized and extreme for popular taste, the breeder hoped to create a cat with some of the qualities she found most attractive in each breed. She thought the Tonkinese, especially those with points and blue eyes, would appeal to people searching for a Siamese of the more old-fashioned style.

blue mink

A New York pet-store owner had been working toward the same goal about ten years earlier. He had called his cats Golden Siamese and the Canadian strain took the same name until it was changed to Tonkinese.

The Tonkinese was first accepted for championship competition by the Canadian Cat Association in 1965 and in the US in 1972. It is now registered with all US associations, but not in all colors and patterns. In Britain, only one association accepts the breed, allowing all the standard recognized Burmese colors. Other countries have yet to appreciate the qualities of this delightful animal.

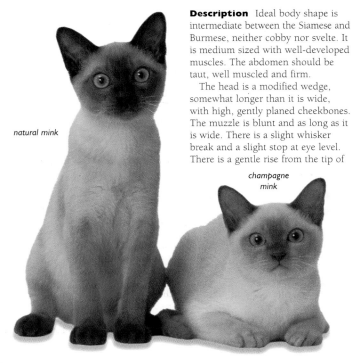

natural mink

champagne mink

Description Ideal body shape is intermediate between the Siamese and Burmese, neither cobby nor svelte. It is medium sized with well-developed muscles. The abdomen should be taut, well muscled and firm.

The head is a modified wedge, somewhat longer than it is wide, with high, gently planed cheekbones. The muzzle is blunt and as long as it is wide. There is a slight whisker break and a slight stop at eye level. There is a gentle rise from the tip of

platinum mink

the nose to the stop and a slight rise from the nose stop to the forehead. The nose leather should harmonize with the coat color.

The open, almond-shaped eyes slant up along the cheekbones toward the outer edges of the ears. Their striking aquamarine to turquoise color is a definitive characteristic of the Tonkinese breed and is seen at its best in natural light. They are the result of combining the blue of the Siamese

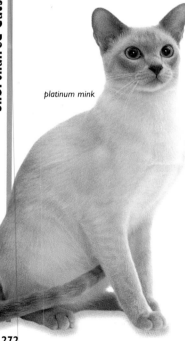

platinum mink

with the gold of the Burmese. The medium-sized ears are covered with very short hair, and are broad at the base with oval tips. They are set as much on the sides of the head as on the top.

The legs are fairly slim and in proportion in length and boning to the body. The paws are more oval than round and the pads should harmonize with the coat color. The long tail tapers to a slender tip and should have no kinks.

The lustrous coat is medium-short in length, fine and silky, and lies close to the body. In the mature animal, the body color should be rich, even and unmarked, shading to a lighter tone on the underparts of the body. There must be a distinct contrast between body color and points, which may darken with age. The points are densely marked on the mask, ears, feet and tail. An occasional combing to remove dead hair, a brush with a rubber brush and a rub over with a damp chamois

champagne mink

is all that is needed to keep the coat in good condition.

Varieties Some associations allow other colors, such as Siamese (pointed, with blue eyes) or Burmese (solid colored, with golden eyes), but the Tonkinese comes in only these five colors for championship showing in the US, either pointed or in solid colors:

Champagne mink: the body is soft, buff cream; the points are medium brown; the nose leather and paw pads are cinnamon brown.

Blue mink: the body is soft blue to blue-gray; the points are slate blue; the nose leather and paw pads are blue-gray.

Honey mink: the body is golden cream, preferably with an apricot cast; the points are light to medium ruddy brown; the nose leather and paw pads are caramel pink.

Natural mink: the body is medium brown; the points are dark brown; the nose leather and paw pads are dark brown.

Platinum mink: the body is pale, silvery gray with warm overtones; the points are frosty gray; the nose leather and paw pads are lavender pink.

Temperament Intelligent, lively and lovable, the Tonkinese is in every way a charmer, with the strong personality and curiosity of the Siamese evident. It dislikes being left alone for long periods of time and can be mischievous if bored or lonely. If you must be absent for hours at a time, consider acquiring two cats so they can keep each other company. Make sure your home is escape-proof before you bring your Tonkinese home as it is adept at finding ways to get out. It is playful, affectionate, healthy, long-lived and easy to look after—what more could anyone want?

blue mink

natural mink

LONGHAIRED CATS

Over the past century or so, breeders have deliberately selected for particular coat characteristics to produce ever-more glamorous and appealing animals. Persians, in particular, have undergone dramatic changes to give us the vast range of colors and coat types available today. Some coats are so dense and plush that running your fingers through them is a sensory pleasure. Because of each shaft's pigment content, some hair colors offer a different texture. For example, white hair is usually soft and silky, blue hair is cottony and dense, and the black, ticked or tabby hairs are often more harsh with a thicker texture. Despite the common factor of being longhaired, each breed is a distinct entity.

AMERICAN CURL

The backward-tipped ears of the American Curl make it unmistakable. Curious and companionable, these attractive cats adapt easily to almost any home situation and tolerate the presence of other animals remarkably well. It comes with either a longhaired and shorthaired coat.

silver ticked shorthair

History Although its history is very brief, this breed has already gathered a growing band of admirers. The first American Curl was a black longhair female kitten of unknown parentage that appeared on the doorstep of Joe and Grace Ruga's home in Lakewood, California, in 1981. Captivated by her unusual ears, they kept her, calling her Shulamith, meaning "black and comely." All American Curls must trace their pedigree to Shulamith, the foundation female.

In December 1981, Shulamith delivered a litter of four kittens, two with the same curly ears as their mother. A geneticist was consulted to study this phenomenon and he confirmed that the unusual ear was a genetic trait and that the gene was dominant.

Selective breeding and presentation in shows of American Curls began in 1983, and they are now accepted in all associations in the US. They enjoy good health and come in all colors and patterns, with both long and short hair. The International Cat Association accepted the breed for registration in 1985 and granted it championship status in 1986. The breed is, as yet, not recognized for showing in Britain.

Description The American Curl's body is medium sized, elongated in shape with moderate strength and tone. The head is a modified wedge, longer than it is wide, with a straight nose and a muzzle that is neither pointed nor square. It is an elegant and alert animal with a sweet and friendly expression. The

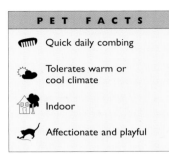

PET FACTS

- Quick daily combing
- Tolerates warm or cool climate
- Indoor
- Affectionate and playful

eyes are walnut shaped, moderately large and may be any color, with no particular relationship to the coat color, except that blue eyes are required in colorpoint classes. Legs are of medium boning and the feet are medium sized and rounded. The tail is wide at the base, tapered and equal in length to

brown classic tabby and white longhair

the body; the longhaired American Curl has a beautiful plumed tail. The outstanding feature of the American Curl is its remarkable curled ears. At birth, the ears are straight but they begin to curl back during the first ten days of life. The degree of curl is not finally established until the kittens are about four months old. Care should always be taken when handling the ears—never force the ear into an unnatural position or you may break the cartilage. The degree of curl to the ears is of paramount importance in show specimens.

red classic tabby longhair

There should be a minimum of 90° arc and a maximum of 180° of curl. The cartilage should be firm from the base of the ear to at least a third of its height. The ears are wide at the base and open, curving back in a smooth arc when viewed from front and rear. The tips must be rounded and flexible.

Since the curl of the ear is the major identifying feature of the American Curl, the standard calls for disqualification of any cat if its ears curl to such an extreme that they touch the back of the ear or head, or if the ears are straight or severely mis-matched in the degree of curl.

The coats of both longhair and shorthair types are soft and silky with minimal undercoat and no ruff. Grooming is easy because the hair does not mat—regular combing and an occasional bath will keep these intriguing cats looking good.

Varieties American Curls come in all colors and patterns. Choose from a glistening snow-white with azure blue eyes, or a silver tabby with emerald-green eyes. Since they have such a wide gene pool (Curls can be mated to any other breed that matches their physical conformation), you can find an American Curl with any color coat, including colorpointed, and any eye color that you wish. Because it is their unique curled ears that set them apart, any color, eye color or coat length is acceptable for the purpose of showing.

Temperament Curious and friendly, the impish American Curl enjoys human company and remains playful and kitten-like throughout its adult life. These cats are very affectionate, even-tempered, lively and intelligent, and quickly make friends with new human acquaintances.

brown spotted shorthair

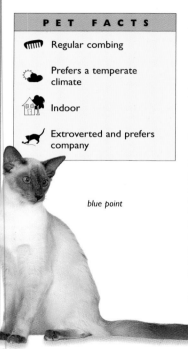

blue point

seal lynx point

PET FACTS

- Regular combing
- Prefers a temperate climate
- Indoor
- Extroverted and prefers company

BALINESE AND JAVANESE

With its gently swaying tail, the Balinese is the epitome of natural grace. It looks regal and aristocratic, like a Siamese in a spectacular pale ermine coat. Intelligence shines in its brilliant sapphire eyes and its inquisitive nature makes it a wonderful pet.

History During the 1930s and 1940s, many Siamese breeders tried to produce a longhaired Siamese by crossing them with Turkish Angoras. Most of the offspring, however, were shorthaired and the breeders gave up. It later became apparent that many of the shorthaired offspring were carrying a recessive longhaired gene and it wasn't long before two such cats were mated and produced a Siamese with a longer coat.

An early champion of the breed proposed the romantic name Balinese for her beloved long-haired Siamese.

Her choice was adopted and these cats have been known as Balinese ever since. The breed gained championship status in the US in 1963.

Description A light-bodied cat, the Balinese is exactly like a Siamese, except for its coat. It has a long tubular body and is sleek, svelte and well muscled. It has fine bones with narrow shoulders and hips, which continue the body's sleek lines. The abdomen should be tight with no evidence of obesity or emaciation.

The head is a long tapering wedge. The nose is long and straight with no break and the nose leather should harmonize with the coat color. The muzzle is fine and wedge-shaped, the chin and jaw must be firm, neither receding nor excessively massive, and the neck should be long and slender.

The deep, vivid blue, almond-shaped eyes slant up from the nose. The ears are strikingly large, pointed, wide at the base and continue the lines of the head's wedge.

The long, slim legs end in dainty, oval paws with the pad color harmonizing with the coat color. The tail is long and thin, tapering to a fine point, with its covering of hair spreading out like a plume.

The coat is medium length rather than long, but may be longer on the underbelly, around the neck and on the tail. The texture is fine and silky, with no downy undercoat. For this reason, the coat does not mat and grooming is simple—regular combing and brushing is enough to maintain its beautiful appearance. While the original Balinese had long

flowing coats, repeated breeding to Siamese to achieve the desired type has lessened the length of the coat. Indeed, you might very well see a Balinese today with nothing more than a few wisps on its belly and a slightly fuller tail to indicate that it is not a Siamese.

Varieties The Balinese is a colorpoint cat and comes in seal point, blue point, lilac point, chocolate point, red point, tortie point and lynx point. The red points, tortie points and lynx points are called "Javanese" by the Cat Fanciers' Association, but Balinese by all other associations.

Temperament
The Balinese is a slightly toned-down version of its Siamese cousin. It is intelligent, active and inquisitive,

but does not have a loud voice. Some of the longhaired ancestors are perhaps responsible for these cats being somewhat less vocal and having softer voices. They dislike being left on their own and can be mischievous if they are bored and lonely. The answer to this could be to have two cats.

chocolate point

lilac point

BIRMAN

A gorgeous cat with sapphire eyes, the Birman is known as the Sacred Cat of Burma. Its long, sumptuous coat and beautiful coloring would be enough to win admirers, but it also has intelligence, good health and a gentle temperament.

lynx point kitten

seal point kitten

seal point

History The origin of the Birman is lost in legend, but it was once considered sacred, a companion cat of the Kittah priests in Burma. Earlier this century, two Birman cats were clandestinely shipped from Burma to France. The male did not survive the long voyage, but the female, Sita, did and, happily, was pregnant. From this small foundation, the Birman was established in the Western world. The French cat registry recognized the Birman as a separate breed in 1925, but Britain did not follow suit until 1966. The breed won recognition in the US in 1967.

Description Ideally, the Birman is long, large and stocky. It has a strong, broad, rounded head with a Roman nose of medium length. The face has a sweet expression, with full cheeks, a somewhat rounded muzzle and a strong chin. The medium-sized ears are set far apart on the head and have rounded tips. The blue eyes are quite round.

The Birman has heavy-boned legs of medium length. Its paws are large and round, and all four are white; these are the Birman's distinguishing feature. The white gloves on the front feet, preferably symmetrical, usually end in an even line across the paw at, or between, the second or third joints. Those on the back paws should cover all the toes and should also extend up the back of the hock (the first joint). These leg markings are called "laces." Ideally, the front gloves match, the back gloves match, and the two laces match. Faultlessly gloved cats are indeed rare and the Birman is judged in all of its parts as well as the gloves. The paw pads are pink or pink spotted with the point color. The tail is bushy and of medium length.

The longhaired, silky hair is not as thick as that of the Persian and doesn't mat if it is brushed regularly to remove dead hair. The pale coat sometimes looks as if it has been

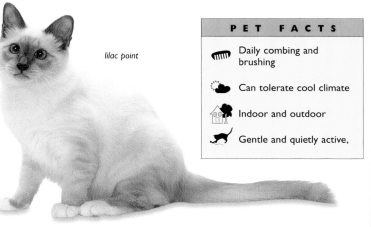

lilac point

PET FACTS

- Daily combing and brushing
- Can tolerate cool climate
- Indoor and outdoor
- Gentle and quietly active,

dusted with gold. The "points"— mask, ears, legs and tail—are darker, like those of the Siamese and the Himalayan.

Varieties The Birman comes in seal point, chocolate point, blue point and lilac point. Recently, some Birmans have appeared in the colors of red point, tortie point and lynx point, but these are not as yet recognized anywhere in the world for championship showing.

Temperament The gentle Birman has a delightful personality and is active, playful and independent. It makes a good pet for children.

blue classic tabby

PET FACTS

- Combing and brushing three times a week
- Can tolerate cold climate
- Indoor and outdoor
- Loving nature and talkative

MAINE COON

Large, powerfully built and impressive, the Maine Coon is healthy, active and good-natured. Whether it becomes a working farm cat, a treasured household companion or a show champion, it will always make its presence felt.

History The Maine Coon, perhaps the earliest American breed, is probably descended from the first domestic cats to arrive on the North American continent. Early this century, these cats fell from favor with most breeders, who preferred to import longhairs with long pedigrees and without the white lockets, or markings on the neck, of the Maine Coons. Eventually, the Maine Coon disappeared from the show bench altogether, but its hardy genes were used to strengthen the Persian breed in the US, to the dismay of the same purists. It was not until the late 1950s that the Maine Coon gained championship status in its own right.

Description One of the largest of all domestic cats, the Maine Coon has a muscular and broad-chested body that is much longer than the other longhaired breeds. Males are much larger and heavier than females. The large head is a broad, modified wedge of medium length with a squared off muzzle. The cheekbones are high. In profile, the medium-length nose is slightly concave. The wide-set eyes are large and expressive, slightly slanted toward the outer base of the ear. They may be green, gold or copper and do not necessarily conform to the coat color. Some white cats may have blue or odd-colored eyes. The ears are large, pointed, well-tufted and wide at the base. They are set moderately well apart and high on the head.

The medium-length legs are rounded, substantial and wide set, and the paws are large, round and well tufted, with pads

silver mackerel tabby and white

that harmonize with the coat. The long tail is wide at the base with long, flowing hair and comes to a blunt end. No kinks are allowed in the tails of show cats.

The lustrous, dense coat of the Maine Coon is shaggy and, with its slight but definite undercoat, heavy enough to protect the animal from a harsh climate. A frontal ruff is desirable. The hair is short on the face and shoulders, but longer on the stomach and hind legs, where it forms britches. The hair falls smoothly, following the lines of the body. Grooming consists of a light brushing every few days to remove dead hair. This should be enough to stop mats from forming.

Varieties This breed comes in all colors and patterns, except colorpointed, solid

red tabby and cream tabby kittens

lilac and solid chocolate. There is often white around the mouth and chin of tabbies.

Temperament The gentle Maine Coon is known for its loving nature, calm disposition and intelligence, and especially for the soft little chirping noises it makes as it goes about its day. It is a delightful companion, loving and loyal and very patient with children. It is an excellent hunter and doesn't hesitate to go into water. It sometimes picks up food with its front paws.

Norwegian Forest Cat

A gorgeous, wild-looking animal, the Norwegian Forest Cat emerged from the forest and opted for domesticity and work on the farm some time during the past 4,000 years. Despite appearances, the coat is easy to care for.

blue and white

brown mackerel tabby and white

History Although highly prized by Norwegian farmers for its superior hunting ability, no one else paid any attention to the Norwegian Forest Cat until the 1930s. The breed almost became extinct during World War II, and owes its survival to Carl-Fredrik Nordane, a former president of the Norwegian Cat Association. In the early 1970s, he organized a breed club to champion and preserve the Forest Cat. The Feline International Federation of Europe (FIFE) granted it championship status in 1977, and the first enchanting specimen arrived in the US two years later. Because of its many similarities to the Maine Coon, it was not recognized there until 1987.

Description The large body is medium length and solidly muscled with substantial bone structure and considerable girth. The chest is broad and the flanks have great depth. The triangular head has a wide, straight nose with no break in the line from brow ridge to tip. The nose leather should harmonize with the coat color. The chin is firm, in line with the front of the nose and gently rounded. The large, almond-shaped eyes are expressive, wide set and have the outer corner slightly higher than the inner. Eye color may be any shade of green, hazel or gold and white cats may have blue or odd eyes. The ears are medium to large, rounded at the tip, upright and set far apart on the head. They do not flare out but follow the line from the side of the head.

The medium-length legs are heavily muscled with thickset lower legs. The paws are large and round and heavily tufted, with pad color in keeping with the coat. The magnificent tail is heavily furred, and remains so even in summer.

The water-resistant double coat is uneven in length with a dense, woolly undercoat and visible guard hairs in winter. The hair on the side of the face flows into a substantial ruff, framing the face like a full beard. The britches should be full. Daily combing is recommended when the winter coat is being shed but, unless it is destined for the show ring, the cat will take care of this itself. Surprisingly, the hair does not mat.

Varieties The Norwegian Forest Cat comes only in longhair. Any color or pattern is acceptable, except colorpointed, solid lilac or chocolate. Popular colors include brown tabby, silver tabby and either of those with white. These colors originally helped the cat to blend into its woodland surroundings.

Temperament While the Norwegian Forest Cat is an excellent hunter and loves the outdoors, it also craves company. It loves to be handled and petted and returns this affection in full measure. As with other breeds, if a kitten is gently handled and exposed to children, cats and dogs from birth, the temperament will be more adaptable than that of one raised with limited human contact.

P E T   F A C T S

Very little combing (except for show specimens)

Can tolerate cold climate

Indoor and outdoor

Companionable and loyal

brown mackerel tabby and white kitten

brown ticked tabby and white

287

PET FACTS

🪮 Thorough daily combing, brushing is essential

☁️ Can tolerate cool climate

🏠 Indoor and outdoor (except for show cats, which must be kept inside to protect the coat

🐈 Loving companions, relatively quiet

cream

PERSIAN

The most popular breed of all in the US, the Persian is prized for its luxurious flowing coat, neat, pretty little face and sweet personality. It now comes in so many patterns and colors that it is almost impossible to choose a favorite. Today's Persian has lost the ability to hunt and fend for itself.

History The long coat of the original Persian was probably a mutation that developed in response to the cold climate, but since this cat became known in Europe in the 1600s, its beauty has been the spur to perfecting the coat. It is believed that the Persian was among the first breeds to be registered and shown, along with the Manx, Abyssinians and Domestic Shorthairs. Originally, they were called Longhairs rather than Persians, and this term was used until the early 1960s in the US. In Britain, they still go by the name Longhairs, and each color is considered a separate breed and may have a slightly different standard.

Today's US Persian came about from matings between the Turkish Angora and the Maine Coon cats. The early influence of the Maine Coon is still very apparent on the show bench, with many silver and tabby Persians retaining the larger and higher-set ears of that ancestor.

With selective breeding and crossing only like colors, great advances were made in the setting of the Persian type. Many of the outstanding blues produced in

Britain in the 1940s and 1950s eventually became the breeding stock of catteries in the US.

These blues are still considered the yardstick by which every other color is judged, and any blue Persian being exhibited must meet or excel in its standard.

Description The ideal Persian is a medium to large cat with a broad, stocky body, cobby in type and low on the legs. The chest is broad and deep, the shoulders and rump equally wide across, with a well-rounded mid-section. The muscles are firm and well developed.

The head is broad and well rounded when viewed from any angle. The forehead is domed with no vertical ridges. The cheeks are full and the nose is short, snub and broad. There is a decided horizontal indentation between the eyes, called the break. The chin is full and well developed in profile, with the chin, nose and forehead in a perpendicular line. The jaws are broad and powerful and the neck is so short and thick that it looks as if the head is sitting directly on top of the shoulders.

The eyes are large, round, brilliant, set level and far apart, and the color must conform to the coat color. The eyes should be cleaned daily as part of the grooming routine. The ears are small, round-tipped, tilted forward and set wide apart. They should not be unduly open at the base, and should fit closely into the rounded contour of the head.

The legs are short, thick and straight with heavy boning. The feet are firm and well rounded, and long tufts between the toes are desirable. The paw pads and nose leather should harmonize with the coat color. The length of the tail should be in proportion to body length,

red

chocolate

tortie point
Himalayan

copper-eyed white kitten

chinchilla silver

with considerable fullness. The thick coat can be up to 6 inches (15 cm) long, and is soft, dense and full of life. There should be a long, full ruff. The main drawback is that the coat must be groomed every day because it sheds year-round and the cat will have problems with matting and hairballs if the dead hair is not removed regularly. Use a metal comb or a brush with long wires or natural bristles for the task. Many owners like to bathe their animals, and there are specific instructions for the care of different colors and coat types for show purposes. Some enthusiasts at shows and professional groomers may be happy to demonstrate the various tricks.

Varieties In Britain, each Longhair color has a slightly different standard for head and body type. In the US, all colors of Persians must compete to the same exacting dictates of the standard, which puts some colors at a disadvantage. It is not as easy to

black smoke

tortoiseshell

divisions in each of which most of the colors can be found. The solid division comprises the whites (blue-eyed, copper-eyed and odd-eyed), creams, blacks, blues, reds, lilacs and chocolates. All the solids, except the whites, must have brilliant copper eyes.

The star of the shaded division is the chinchilla silver. This is a pure white cat with delicate black tipping on the ends of the hairs, brick red nose leather, and blue-green eyes. In the US, there is also a Shaded Silver class that calls for heavier black tipping and dark mascara markings on the face, but in Britain, there is only one class of silvers.

Other lovely colors in the shaded division include goldens, cameos (white cats with red tipping), as well as chinchilla and shaded versions of all of the solid colors. Eyes must be copper, except for the silvers with blue-green eyes, and the goldens, which have green to hazel eyes.

Next comes the smoke division, with such colors as cream smoke, black smoke, blue smoke, cameo smoke, lilac smoke, chocolate smoke and tortoiseshell smoke. This class calls for a solid white cat so heavily tipped on its outer hair with one of the above colors that it looks like a solid colored cat. The breathtaking beauty of the smoke is apparent when you blow softly down the

shaded cameo

produce a silver Persian with the same head type and ear set as most of the other colors. In the US, pointed colors are called Himalayan Persians in most associations, although in some they are still classified solely as Himalayans and judged as a separate breed. In Britain, they are called Colorpoint Longhairs.

As well as being classified by color, Persians are further separated into

calico

back and the hair parts to reveal the snowy white undercoat. The smoke usually has copper eyes and a luxurious white ruff framing its face.

The tabby division consists of cream tabby, brown tabby, blue tabby, red tabby, chocolate tabby, lilac tabby, silver tabby, cameo tabby and torbie (patched tabby). Each of these comes in four tabby patterns, classic (or blotched), ticked, mackerel or spotted. The tabby patterns should be clearly distinguishable from the ground color and, except for the silver tabby, all eye color must be copper. These cats are quite striking in appearance. The tortoiseshell division is the smallest and is composed of blue creams, lilac creams, chocolate creams and tortoiseshell (red and black). The pattern comprises of the two

red and white

*brown
classic tabby*

colors splotched randomly over the cat. A dividing mark down the nose and under the chin (called a "blaze") is desirable. The eyes should be copper colored.

The particolor (also called bicolor) division is made up of calicos—a white cat with red and black splotches—that are also called tortoiseshell and white, as well as a lilac calico, a blue calico, a chocolate calico, and any of the solid, smoke, tortoiseshell, shaded or tabby colors with the addition of white. The eyes should be a brilliant copper to orange color.

The newest division (in most associations) is the Himalayan. This covers colorpoint Persians that are lilac point, blue point, chocolate point, seal point, red point, tortie point and lynx point. The tortie and lynx points may be seal, blue, lilac or chocolate. All Himalayans must have blue eyes.

Temperament Calm and gentle, the Persian is a lovable and appealing animal. It is hard to resist that little face, almost lost in fur, and fortunately, this cat enjoys being admired, petted and pampered. It will pose, draping itself on a windowsill or chair almost like a piece of art. It has a quiet, melodious voice and responds to stroking with delighted little chirps and murmurs. The large eyes are also most expressive of contentment. The Persian enjoys company but is not demanding in this respect and is quite capable of entertaining itself while you are out of the house for a few hours without tearing the place apart. These cats have a quality of great stillness and serenity and will sometimes sit for long periods doing absolutely nothing except looking beautiful, which is more than enough for most of their doting owners.

chocolate point Himalayan

blue cream point Himalayan

293

RAGDOLL

The Ragdoll is so named because of its ability to relax totally, like a ragdoll, when handled. This, along with its intelligence, even temperament and devotion to its owners, makes the Ragdoll a great pet for families with children.

seal mitted

blue mitted

History The Ragdoll was developed in California during the 1960s from a white longhair and a seal point Birman. Subsequently, Burmese was added to the mix. The breed has been surrounded in controversy ever since, and although recognized for championship showing in 1965, it has yet to achieve that status with the Cat Fanciers' Association (CFA), the largest cat association in the US. It has recently been recognized in Britain but not as yet in many other countries. One of the controversial claims made for the Ragdoll is that it does not feel pain, but this certainly has no basis. The Ragdoll's habit of lying relaxed and unprotesting when it is being handled may have led to this misconception.

Description The ideal Ragdoll has a large, well-boned, muscular and substantial body, somewhat elongated. It is massive across the shoulders and chest and heavy in the hindquarters with a tendency to develop a "fatty pad" on the lower abdomen. The head is a broad modified wedge with the appearance of a flat plane between the ears. The medium-length muzzle is round, with a well-developed chin. The medium-length nose has a break between the eyes and the leather harmonizes with the coat. The neck is short, heavy and strong. The large oval eyes are sapphire blue, wide set and in line with the base of the ear. The medium-sized ears are wide at the base with rounded tips. They are set to gently cup the skull and continue the wedge shape.

The strong-boned legs are medium to medium-long, with the back legs longer than the front. The fur on the front legs is short and thick, while that on the hind legs is medium to long, thick and feathery. The paws are large, round and feather-tufted with pad colors that harmonize with the coat. The tail is long, fluffy and in proportion to body length.

The plush, silky coat is medium-long to long, being longest around the neck and outer edges of the face. Although the fur is non-matting, the coat must be combed daily with a wide-toothed comb to remove tangles and dead hair, then brushed gently with a long-bristled brush. This is especially important when the

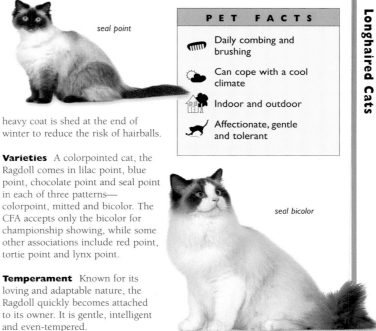

seal point

heavy coat is shed at the end of winter to reduce the risk of hairballs.

Varieties A colorpointed cat, the Ragdoll comes in lilac point, blue point, chocolate point and seal point in each of three patterns—colorpoint, mitted and bicolor. The CFA accepts only the bicolor for championship showing, while some other associations include red point, tortie point and lynx point.

Temperament Known for its loving and adaptable nature, the Ragdoll quickly becomes attached to its owner. It is gentle, intelligent and even-tempered.

seal bicolor

PET FACTS

- Daily combing and brushing
- Can cope with a cool climate
- Indoor and outdoor
- Affectionate, gentle and tolerant

🪮 Daily grooming

☁ Can tolerate a cool climate

🏡 Indoor and outdoor

🐈 Quietly affectionate and well adjusted

calico

SCOTTISH FOLD

The unusual ears of this gentle cat can give it the inquiring and charming look of a barn owl. Although not the result of a deliberate crossing, the Scottish Fold has already become one of the ten most popular cats in the US.

History Although kittens with this type of genetic mutation have probably been appearing for a long time, the first Fold we know anything about was discovered in the litter of a farm cat near Coupar Angus in the Tayside Region of Scotland in 1961. She was a white cat named Susie. All of today's Folds are Susie's descendants.

Two Folds should never be bred together because of the danger of rigidity of the tail and stiffness in the hind legs in the kittens. Because Folds are often bred with American or British Shorthairs in the US and with British Shorthairs in Britain, the two types are now distinctly different in head type and coat texture. The gene for the folded ears is dominant,

so some kittens in each litter will have them, but not all. The breed is still unrecognized by the Governing Council of the Cat Fancy of Britain because of concern over possible cartilage defects, but it holds championship status with the Cat Association of Britain and was granted championship status in the US in 1978.

Description The stocky, medium-sized body is well padded, rounded and proportioned evenly from shoulder to pelvis. Preference in type seems to lean toward the British Shorthair crossing. The head of this crossing is well rounded and the muzzle has well-rounded whisker pads; the head should blend into a short neck. The cheeks are prominent with a jowly appearance in the males. The large, well-rounded eyes are wide open with a sweet expression and are separated by a broad nose. Their color usually corresponds to the coat color. The broad nose is short with a gentle curve and a brief stop is permitted, although a definite nose break is a fault. The nose leather should match the coat color.

cream mackerel tabby

The ears are this cat's distinguishing feature and should fold forward and downward and sit like a cap on the rounded head. A smaller, tightly folded ear is preferred over one that is loosely folded and large. The ear tips are rounded. (Scottish Folds are no more prone to ear infections than cats with conventional ears.)

There must be no hint of thickness in the legs or lack of mobility due to short, coarse legs. The paws are neat and round, with pads to harmonize with coat color. The tapered tail is of medium length. In judging, the tail should be gently manipulated to make sure it is flexible and not rigid.

The coat comes in both long and shorthaired versions and should be dense and resilient. Regular brushing will remove dead hair and keep the coat in good condition.

Varieties The Scottish Fold comes in all colors and patterns, except solid lilac, chocolate and colorpointed.

Temperament With its mixture of British and American Shorthair ancestors, the Fold has the best traits of both breeds. It loves human companionship, is placid and very affectionate and easily adjusts to other pets. A hardy cat with a sweet disposition, it has a tiny voice and is not very vocal.

white

297

SELKIRK REX

A well-proportioned cat, the Selkirk Rex is being developed from a spontaneous genetic mutation that appeared only a decade ago. As yet, this good-natured cat is little known outside the US, but it seems certain to win hearts.

black smoke shorthair

cream point shorthair

red classic tabby shorthair

History This is the most recent of the Rex variations to appear. The first cat with this naturally curled coat was found in 1987 in Wyoming, USA, and the type has already been accepted for championship competition by all US associations. The original cat was crossed with a purebred black Persian and three of the six kittens in the resulting litter were curly coated, so it seems that the curls are associated with a dominant gene. Persians, Exotic Shorthairs and British and American Shorthairs are among the breeds that have contributed to the makeup of this attractive cat. Buyers should be aware, however, that this is still a very new breed, so genetic weaknesses associated with its genes may yet be discovered.

Description The Selkirk Rex is being developed as a large, heavy-boned cat, rather like the British Shorthair in conformation. The substantial, muscular torso is rectangular and the back is straight. The shoulders and hips should be the same width. The head is round, broad and full-cheeked with no flat planes. In profile, the nose has a stop or moderate break, and the nose leather is in harmony with the coat color. The chin is firm and well developed, and both male and female have definite jowls. The eyes are large, rounded and set well apart. The eye color need not conform to coat color. The medium-sized ears are pointed and set well apart.

The medium-length legs are well-boned, being neither short and cobby nor long and lanky. The large paws are round and firm, with pads that harmonize with the coat color.

The coat is considerably longer than the other Rex breeds, with definite guard hairs. It is soft, plush, full and obviously curly, with the soft feel of lambswool. The hair is arranged in loose, individual curls that may be more evident around the neck, on the tail and on the belly. If the coat is combed every few days with a wide-toothed comb, it will remove dead hair and help the cat to maintain the coat in good condition. For showing,

spritz the coat with water between judgings to bring out the curl—this works better than combing. Too much combing and brushing of a wet coat will straighten the hairs and the curl will be less obvious.

Varieties All colors and patterns are acceptable, including solid lilac, chocolate, tabby and colorpointed.

Temperament Healthy, sturdy and incredibly patient, the Selkirk Rex has a loving, tolerant disposition.

red longhair

brown tabby longhair

PET FACTS

Light regular combing

Can tolerate cool weather

Indoor and outdoor

Sturdy and affectionate, extremely patient

SIBERIAN

A magnificent, wild-looking cat, the Siberian is an excellent hunter and is well adapted to surviving in a climate of extreme temperatures. Little is known of its background, but some people think that it is one of the earliest longhaired breeds.

brown mackerel tabby

cream mackerel tabby

History Siberian Forest Cats are not common outside Russia, but in their homeland, they are an ancient breed. The first cats of this breed to be imported to the US from Russia arrived in 1990 and they are already attracting a great deal of attention.

They have also been shown in championship competition in Europe. At present, Siberian forest cats are not accepted in the US by the Cat Fanciers' Association, although they can be shown in the other associations.

Description A large, strong, well-muscled cat, the Siberian differs from the Maine Coon and Norwegian Forest cats in that the general impression is one of roundness and circles rather than wedges and angles. Its body is moderately long and substantial, with the back slightly curved or arched. The mature body should have an overall sausage shape with tight muscles and large bones.

The head is a modified wedge of medium size with well-rounded contours, broader at the skull and narrowing slightly to a full, rounded muzzle and a well-rounded chin. The cheekbones are neither set high nor prominent. The top of the head is flat and the nose curves slightly in a gentle slope. The nose pad is a color that harmonizes with the coat. The eyes are large, expressive and almost round. They are set wide with the outer corner angled toward the inner base of the ear. Although the eyes are usually golden-green, any eye color is allowed and it need not conform to the coat color. The medium-large ears are broad at the base and set far apart. Tufts of hair on the tips of the ears are desirable.

The legs are moderately long with heavy bones. The paws are large and rounded and toe tufts are desirable. The paw pads are a color in keeping with the coat. The tail is medium length, wide at the base and blunt at the tip, with abundant hair.

On the body, the double coat is moderately long to long, with a dense, paler undercoat and full ruff. The thick coat is quite specialized to protect the animal from extremes of cold in its native land and the oily guard hairs make it water resistant

and able to shed snow easily. The coat does not mat, but light, regular grooming is recommended, especially during spring and summer, when the heavy winter coat is shed. This will help to prevent hairballs developing.

Varieties The Siberian cat comes only as a longhair. Although brown tabby is the most common color, it may be any pattern or color or combination of colors, except colorpoint, solid lilac or solid chocolate. The longer hairs are pale near the skin, darkening toward the outer end. This makes the coat shimmer as the cat moves.

Temperament The Siberian cat has a sweet personality to go with the sweet expression on its face. It is robust, and makes a loving, gentle and faithful companion.

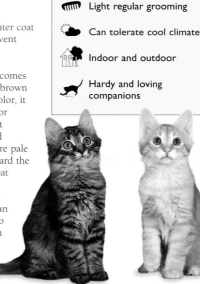

PET FACTS

- Light regular grooming
- Can tolerate cool climate
- Indoor and outdoor
- Hardy and loving companions

brown tabby

cream tabby

301

SOMALI

With its beautiful coat of many colors, the agile Somali is enjoying a meteoric rise to fame and popularity. It makes a delightful and entertaining pet.

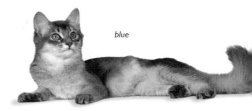

blue

ruddy

History A longhaired version of the Abyssinian, the Somali was developed from longhaired kittens that appeared in the litters of Abyssinians carrying the gene for long hair. (Somalis, conversely, never produce shorthaired kittens.)

The Somali Cat Club of America was founded in 1972 and recognition for championship showing was soon gained from the now-defunct National Cat Fanciers' Association. Somalis are now accepted for championship showing in all US associations and are becoming increasingly popular throughout the world, although not all of the glorious coat colors are accepted for show purposes.

Description The medium-long body is lithe and graceful with strong, well-developed muscles. The rib cage is rounded and the back is slightly arched, which makes it look as if the cat is about to spring. Its structure strikes a balance between cobby and svelte.

The head is a modified, slightly rounded wedge, without flat planes; the brow, cheek and profile lines all showing a gentle contour. The almond-shaped eyes are large, brilliant and expressive, either gold, green or hazel, with deeper shades preferred. They are accented by dark lids and above each eye is a short, dark vertical stroke; dark horizontal strokes continue from the upper lid toward the ear. The large, moderately pointed ears are broad and cupped at the base. They are medium-set toward the back of the head. The inner ear should have horizontal tufts that reach nearly to the other side of the ear and tufts on the tips of the ears are desirable.

The legs are in proportion to the torso and the oval feet are small, with tufted toes. The paw pads vary with the coat color. The tail has a full brush, is thick at the base and tapers to a slender tip.

The double, medium-length coat is very soft, extremely fine and the denser the better. It doesn't mat, but should be combed regularly to remove dead hair. Preference is given to those cats with a ruff and britches, giving a full-coated appearance. Any white must be confined to the upper throat, chin or nostrils.

Varieties The Somali comes in red, ruddy, blue and fawn. The hair is ticked everywhere, except on the underside of the body, but the ticking is not fully developed until the cat is about 18 months old. Each hair may have as many as three distinct bands. The chest, inside of the legs and belly must be clear of markings. A faint broken necklace, although not desirable, is acceptable. However, a dark unbroken necklace would cause disqualification in a show specimen.

Temperament Intelligent, extroverted and very sociable, the Somali has a zest for life, loves to play, and thrives on human companionship. It likes to spend time outdoors and may be restless if confined. It has a soft voice, but is not usually very vocal.

PET FACTS

🪮 Daily brushing

☁ Can tolerate cool weather

🏘 Indoor and outdoor

🐈 Playful, active and needs human companionship

red

fawn

odd-eyed white

PET FACTS

🪮 Regular combing

☁️ Tolerates cool weather

🏠 Indoor and outdoor

🐈 Lively, friendly and playful

TURKISH ANGORA

A cat with the most luxurious appearance, the ravishing Turkish Angora can truly be called a Turkish delight. One of the oldest longhaired breeds, strenuous efforts are being made in its homeland to maintain the purity of its bloodlines.

History The Turkish Angora is a pure, natural type that was probably domesticated by the Tartars. These cats became established in Turkey, where they were, and still are, highly regarded. In the sixteenth century, they were presented as gifts to European nobility by Turkish sultans. Since the 1940s, they have been protected and the Ankara Zoo has maintained a breeding colony of Angora cats, breeding only white cats. Although Angoras were known as far back as the 1890s, the Turkish Angora as we know it today did not reach the US until 1962, when two were imported from Turkey's Ankara Zoo.

Description The ideal Turkish Angora is a lithe, balanced, graceful animal with a muscular, medium-sized body—overall balance and fineness of bone are more important than size. The torso is long and slender and the shoulders are the same width as the hips. The small to medium head is wedge-shaped, with a long, gently pointed nose. The nose leather is pink in the white Angora

red classic tabby

and should harmonize with the coat in other colors. The neck is long and slim. No break or hint of a break is allowed in the line of the nose. The large, almond-shaped eyes slant up slightly and have an open expression.

The eyes can be any color with no relationship between eye color and coat color. White cats with odd eyes are prized for reasons of rarity. The large ears are wide at the base, pointed and tufted. They are set high on the head, vertical and erect.

The legs are long and sturdy, with small, round, dainty toes, preferably with tufts of hair in between. The paw pads are pink in the white Angora, but in keeping with the coat in other colors. The tail is long and plumed, tapering from a wide base to a narrow end.

The fine, dense, silky, medium-length coat shimmers with every movement. It is not fully developed until the cat is about two years old.

There is no undercoat and the hair is mainly straight, but wavy on the stomach. There is a long ruff and britches, with longer hair under the body than on the back. The coat should be combed regularly with a medium-toothed comb to remove dead hair and prevent matting. In order to avoid hairballs, grooming is very important when the winter coat is being shed during spring.

Varieties The original Turkish Angora was accepted only in white, with either blue, copper, green, amber or odd eyes. Although they are now registered in all colors and patterns, except colorpoint, solid lilac and chocolate, the majority of breeders still prefer to breed the original white cats.

Temperament Turkish Angoras make wonderful pets and are thought to be among the most intelligent of breeds. They are gentle and friendly, with great charm.

black and white bicolor

silver patched tabby and white

TURKISH VAN

The most unusual characteristic of the Turkish Van is that it has no reluctance to enter the water. It may have become so adapted because of a necessity to catch fish, but it now seems to swim for sheer pleasure, as many dogs do.

red and white

calico

tortie and white

History The founding members of the Turkish Van breed were two kittens taken to England from the Lake Van district in Western Turkey in 1955 by two British women on holiday there. They imported two more Van cats in 1959 and by 1969 the breed was accepted for championship competition in Britain. The following year, the first Vans officially arrived in the US and they were registered there in 1985. Not all associations accept them yet for championship showing.

Although named after Lake Van, there is no evidence that the cats originated there. Armenian people who live around the lake and pronounce "Van" to rhyme with "Don," may have brought these swimming cats with them when they settled in the region.

Description The Van is a solidly built cat with a very broad chest. Its strength and power are apparent in its thick-set body and legs. Mature males should exhibit marked muscular development in the neck and shoulders with the shoulders at least as broad as the head. There is a well-rounded ribcage and muscular hips. The head is a large, broad wedge, with gentle contours, a medium-length nose and prominent cheekbones. In profile, the nose has a slight dip below eye level. The nose leather is pink. The large, round eyes are slightly drawn out at the corners and set on a slant. They should be clear, alert and expressive and have pink rims. The moderately large ears are set fairly high and well apart. The tips are slightly rounded and the insides should be well feathered.

The legs are moderately long and muscular and set wide apart, tapering to rounded, somewhat large feet with tufts between the toes and pink paw pads. The tail is long, full and bushy.

The semi-longhaired coat has a texture like cashmere, soft to the roots with no trace of undercoat. For this reason, it dries quickly after the cat has been for a swim. There is feathering on the ears, legs, feet and belly. Facial fur is short, but there is a frontal neck ruff that becomes more prominent with age. Combing twice a week to remove dead hair will keep the coat looking good, but give it extra attention when the heavy winter coat is being shed to avoid hairballs.

Varieties The Turkish Van comes only in white, and in one pattern, van. This means that only the head and tail are colored and there can be no more than two spots on its body. The color may be solid, cream or auburn in Britain, but in the US, tabby and particolor are also allowed. A blaze or white streak up the nose to at least between the front edge of the ears is very desirable—to the Turks, it signifies the blessing of Allah.

Temperament This cat has an unusually melodious voice, is active and intelligent, and makes a lively companion to the right owner. It is not a lap-cat and will feel more secure, and be easier to handle, when all of its four feet are on a solid surface.

P E T   F A C T S

Regular grooming

Can tolerate cool climate

Indoor and outdoor

Agile, alert and companionable

black and white

Glossary

GLOSSARY

altered a cat that has had its reproductive organs removed (either spayed females or neutered males).

banding distinct bands of color in a cross-wise direction.

bay rum spirit a liquid, once made from bayberry leaves and now made

from a mixture of oils, alcohol and water, helpful in removing stains.

bib the part of the ruff, or lengthened hair, around the chest area.

bicolor a cat with more than two spots of color on the torso, either white and one basic color, or white with one tabby color.

blaze a marking down the forehead, nose and under the chin.

boric-acid powder a white powder used as a mild antiseptic or preservative.

break an indentation at the bridge of the nose, between the eyes or just below the eyes. It is more visible than a stop.

britches long hairs on the back of the hind legs which run from the hips to the hock, or lower joint, of the leg.

calico van a white cat with two spots on the torso in two basic colors.

cat fancier a person involved in breeding, selling and showing cats, usually pedigreed cats.

cat fancy the hobby of breeding, selling and showing cats, usually pedigreed cats.

cattery the place where a breeding cat is kept, either in the home or in a separate outbuilding.

cobby sturdy, round and compact body shape. The body is usually set low on the legs, with broad shoulders and rump.

colorpoint a cat with darker shadings on its mask, ears, paws and tail.

colostrum the milky fluid that is secreted from the mother's nipples, or mammary glands, for the first few days after birth. It is rich in protein and contains antibodies that help protect the young from disease during the first few weeks of their lives.

cornstarch a fine, powdery starch made from corn, rice or other grain. It is known as cornflour in Britain.

double coat a coat of double thickness. Unlike regular coats, the skin is not visible when the coat is parted.

euthanasia to put down, or cause death, in a painless and peaceful manner so as to end incurable illness and suffering.

feral cat an untamed domestic cat that was born, or has reverted to living in the wild.

flanks the fleshy sides of the cat between the ribs and the hips.

gene part of the chromosome from which hereditary traits are determined.

ground color the basic (or lighter) color of the cat in any of the tabby patterns.

guard hairs coarse, long, stiff, protective hairs that form a cat's outer coat.

hand grooming light stroking of the coat with the hand to remove dead hair.

hereditary traits/genes passed down from parents to offspring.

hock first, or lower, joint at the back of the legs.

household pet category If you were entering your mixed-breed cat in a US show, he would be entered in this category.

in season period of time when the female, or queen, is willing to mate with the male, or studcat. Also referred to as estrus or in heat.

inoculation the injection of a vaccine to create immunity. A small amount of a specific disease is injected enabling antibodies to build up and so prevent the occurrence of the disease.

kink a twist, curl, bend or bump in the tail bone.

laces white markings on the legs.

locket solid white marking on the neck.

mackerel a type of tabby pattern where the colors of the coat appear striped.

mask the darker shadings on the face.

mineral spirits turpentine or paint thinner, helpful in removing stains.

mixed-breed a cat comprised of two or more different breeds, which do not combine to make a separate breed; not purebred.

GLOSSARY continued

mutation a variation in a genetic characteristic that is passed on to following generations. It is either accidental or environmental and can be harmless or defective.

muzzle the jaws and mouth.

necklace bandings of color across the lower neck and chest area, as if the cat is actually wearing a necklace.

neuter to surgically remove the testicles of a male cat to prevent reproduction.

odd-eyed having different colored eyes, usually one eye is blue and the other is copper or yellow.

particolor comprising two colors, always white with one other basic color.

pedigree the line of direct descent or ancestry, or the certificate stating the descent or ancestry.

points extremities of the body comprising the mask, ears, legs and tail.

points (show) the score awarded to a cat depending on how the judge rates them according to the standard. A total of 100 points can be awarded by a judge.

pound rescue center or shelter for stray or unwanted animals.

purebred a cat that has been bred from only cats of the same breed so as to produce the same characteristics and traits of previous generations.

quarantine a period of isolation to prevent the spread of a disease. Every country has its own regulations regarding the length of this period.

queen an unaltered female cat.

Roman nose a nose with a lump on it.

rough-housing behaving in a very boisterous, rough or rowdy manner.

ruff protruding or lengthened hair around the neck and chest.

spay to surgically remove the uterus of a female cat to prevent reproduction.

spraying a natural instinct of urinating on surfaces as a means of marking territory. It is most common in the unaltered male cat but unaltered females and altered cats can also spray.

standards guidelines set out for each breed by all associations; they list the qualities that the breed will be judged on in the show ring.

stop a slight indentation at the bridge of the nose, between the eyes or just below the eyes. It is not as visible as a break.

studcat an unaltered male cat, also known as a tomcat.

tabby patterned coat with circular, striped or blotchy markings.

tartar a hard, brownish deposit on the teeth that can cause decay.

ticked dark and light colors on the hair shaft, in alternate bands.

ticking light hairs that are scattered among darker colored hairs or spatterings of lighter hairs among darker colored hairs.

tomcat an unaltered male cat, also known as a studcat.

torbie a combination of the tortoiseshell and the tabby pattern, also called "patched tabby."

tortie abbreviation of tortoiseshell.

tortoiseshell a patched or mottled pattern that can resemble some turtles and tortoises.

unaltered an intact male or female with full reproductive abilities.

undercolor the color of the hair closest to the skin.

van having one or two spots on torso. The spots are one of the basic colors.

walnut-shaped eyes eyes that are oval or almond-shaped on top and round on the bottom.

whisker break an indentation in the upper jaw.

whisker pads the thickened, or fatty pads around the whisker area.

INFORMATION DIRECTORY

The following organizations will be able
to supply you with information on local
contacts from whom to obtain details
on registration, standards, cat shows
and any other information required.

USA

American Cat Association
8101 Katherine Avenue
Panorama City CA 91402
Tel: 818 781 5656
Fax: 818 781 5340

Cat Fanciers' Association
PO Box 1005
Manasquan
NJ 08736-0805
Tel: 732 528 9797
Fax: 732 528 7391

**American Cat Fanciers'
Association**
Branson
MO 65726
Tel: 417 334 5430
Fax: 417 334 5540

CANADA

Canadian Cat Association
220 Advance B1 Ste 101
Brampton
Ontario L6T 4J5
Tel: ++1 905 459 1481
Fax: ++1 905 459 4023

EUROPE

Governing Council of Cat Fancy
4–6 Penel Orlieu
Bridgwater
Somerset TA6 3PG
England
Tel: ++44 1278 427575

Cat Association of Britain
The British member of the FIFe
Mill House
Letcomb Regis
Oxon OX12 9JD
England
Tel: ++44 1235 766543

AUSTRALIA

New South Wales Cat
Fanciers Association Inc.
PO Box 485
Round Corner
Dural
NSW 2158
Tel/ Fax: ++61 2 9634 1822
Email: nswcfa@hotkey.net.au

Feline Control Council
of Victoria
Royal Showgrounds
Epsom Road
Ascot Vale
VIC 3032
Tel: ++61 3 9281 7404
Fax: ++61 3 9376 2973

INDEX

Page references in *italics* indicate illustrations and photos.

INDEX continued

INDEX continued

ACKNOWLEDGMENTS

TEXT Susan Lumpkin, Susie Page, Puddingburn Publishing Services (index), John Seidensticker
ILLUSTRATIONS Alistair Barnard, Janet Jones, Frank Knight PHOTOGRAPHS Ad-Libitum/Stuart Bowey,
Animals Unlimited, Auscape International, Chanan Photography/Richard Katris, Corel Corporation,
Graham Meadows Photography CONSULTANT EDITOR Dr. Paul McGreevy is a veterinarian and lecturer
in animal behavior at the University of Sydney, Australia